CW01019737

The Sands of Dee

Legends and Traditions of the Wirral Peninsula

GAVIN CHAPPELL

DEDICATION

For everyone on the *Hidden Wirral — Myths and Legends*
Facebook page.

Hidden Wirral Myths & Legends

CONTENTS

	Introduction	7
1	The Sands of Dee	12
2	From Chester to Little Stanney	15
3	Netherpool	17
4	Brimstage	20
5	Poulton Lancelyn	24
6	Bromborough	27
7	Bebington	34
8	Storeton	41
9	Prenton	48
10	Landican and Woodchurch	50
11	Birkenhead	52
12	Wallasey	57
13	Bidston	86
14	Meols and Hoylake	96
15	Overchurch	106
16	Greasby	108
17	West Kirby and Hilbre	109

18	Frankby	120
19	Thurstaston	124
20	Barnston	136
21	Heswall	139
22	Gayton	143
23	Neston and Parkgate	147
24	Willaston	151
25	Puddington	153
26	Great Saughall	156
27	Return to Chester	165
28	Wirral in Medieval Legend	166
	Appendices	205

INTRODUCTION: WHEN SQUIRRELS LEAPT FROM TREE TO TREE

From Blacon Point to Hilbre
A squirrel could leap from tree to tree.

-Old saying

In ancient times Wirral was a forest. According to the old rhyme, trees grew all the way from Blacon Point near Chester to the tidal island of Hilbre at the mouth of the Dee Estuary, or in a version recorded in Leasowe Castle, from *Birkenheven* (Birkenhead) to Hilbre. In yet another tradition, recorded in Henry Robinson's legendary account of Wallasey, a man—not a squirrel this time!—'...*might have gone out of treetops from the Meoles to Birkenhead, a token whereof in finding of large tree tops when getting of turves, which roots lyes a great way in the sea at this Present.*'

It seems that this legend was inspired by fossil trees discovered by peat-cutters in the Birket valley and Bidston Moss, and the more famous 'Meolse Stocks' or Petrified Forest at Meols, now no longer visible even at low tide, but once a local landmark; tree stumps and tree roots that vanished into the sea, and were believed to have stretched as far as the similar petrified forest at Formby. Indeed, another rhyme states that:

The squirrels ran from tree to tree
From Formby Point to Hilbre.

Other legends say that the forest once extended as far as Ireland.

Stories of a sunken land off the coast are common in Britain, for example, the more famous Cornish legend of Lyonesse, which seems to have been inspired by the petrified forest in the waters near St. Michael's Mount, still occasionally to be seen at low water, or the Welsh story of Cantre'r Gwaelod, the Low Hundred, said to have been where Cardigan Bay is now.

Certainly, in historical times Wirral extended further than it does now, and there is strong evidence of a significant port at Meols in the Middle Ages and as far back as the Iron Age, since swallowed up by the sea. Gravestones have been found beneath the water off Leasowe Lighthouse and stories speak of a bell that can be heard from the waves, from a church that sank in medieval times. Remains of prehistoric fauna such as Irish Elk and aurochs discovered in the nineteenth century suggest that the submarine forest itself dates as far back as the Old Stone Age.

It was said that while land extended between Meols and Formby, the Mersey flowed into the Dee via the Backford Gap, just north of Chester. In the days of King Arthur, earthquakes and violent inundations of the sea created its new course, formerly known also as the Cheshire Waters, or Mersey Water, and even today often referred to as 'The Water.' Other traditions suggest that Bidston Moss once lay under the sea, Wallasey was an island (the name means 'island of the Welsh,' or, according to some interpretations, 'island of strangers'), Caldy Hill was surrounded by water (Caldy comes from the Old Norse for 'cold island,') and Overchurch was 'the church on the shore.'

The North Wirral coast has certainly been contracting throughout recorded history, with the loss of the once-vibrant port at Meols, which seems to have flourished until the days of the Black Death. The previously mentioned graveyard beneath the waves near Leasowe Lighthouse suggests another lost village, even a lost parish.

Not only is the Wirral Peninsula geographically smaller than it once was, as a political entity, Wirral is a fragment of former greatness. The first reference to Wirral appears in the *Anglo-Saxon Chronicle*'s entry for the year 893 AD, when a Viking army led by a Dane named Hastein took refuge in 'a deserted city in Wirral called Chester.' It seems that in those days Wirral included the city. In the days of Henry VIII, however, traditions recorded by royal antiquary John Leland stated that Wirral began 'two bow-shots north' of Chester's suburbs. In the intervening centuries, when Wirral had come under the sway of more Vikings, then in Norman times become a haunt of outlaws, it had shrunk.

Worse was to come in 1974, when what had once been the Hundred of Wirral, a subdivision of Cheshire, was divided between Cheshire itself and the new county of Merseyside. Since then, Wirral has usually been used to refer to the Metropolitan Borough of Wirral, a part of Merseyside that continues to exist to this day, despite the abolition of Merseyside in the 1980s. Wirral is now a twilight zone lying between Cheshire and the former Merseyside.

Since this book concerns Wirral's traditions, the traditional meaning of Wirral, corresponding with the Hundred, will be used. A final note on nomenclature: 'Wirral' is regarded as the correct usage; 'the Wirral' (short for 'the Wirral Peninsula,' which is correct) is seen as a solecism. Wirral, which comes from the Old English *Wirhealum*, meaning 'meadow of bog myrtle', was known to the Celts as *Cilgwri,* or the Corner.

The following description of the Hundred of Wirral was compiled by William Webb, Under Sheriff to Sir Richard Lea, of Lea and of Denhall, in 1615-1616, and published in King's *Vale Royal.*

I have laboured to cast the Hundred of Wirral by the dimensions thereof into some resemblance, and though, geometrically considered, it comes nearest to the figure of a long square, or rather a rhomboide, yet because the long sides are not straight lines, nor the opposite ends equal in their distance, we must take it, as it is, irregular; and the nearest resemblance that I can give it, is the sole of a lady's left foot pantofle, for the furthest north-west end, compassed with the sea, falls somewhat round; then it narrows itself both ways, and between Bebbington on the east, and Oldfield on the west side, falls narrow of the sole; then it widens itself either way to Stanney, on the one side, and Burton on the other, where it is broadest; then narrowing again till it points with the tip of the toe upon Chester liberties. The Welch Britons call it Killgurry, because it is an angle. That it was in old time a forest, I think cannot be doubted, but that it should not be inhabited, or disforested, till Edward the Third's time, that I suppose to be true but in part; for the very antiquity of the church, some castles, monasteries, and the very manurage of the most part of it yet appearing argue, the contrary.

But I will not contend, for it sufficeth me that I can boast in behalf of the inhabitants there now, and of their industrious predecessors too, that it is at present one of the most fertile parts, and comparable, if not exceeding, any other so much in quantity of the whole county besides. And this will our weekly market of Chester for corn and fish make good for me, and if I add flesh too, I should not miss it much.

To proceed with the description of it, I shall need to lead you but one walk over the length of it, and back again, which I will covenant to dispatch with much brevity, if I may in my walk make some indentures on either hand, as these jovial fellows we see sometimes do, when, coming out of the Tavern, they indent their journies down the street, to survey their friends on either side.

Let's join Webb on his antiquarian stroll around the peninsula. Along the way, we'll learn some more of Wirral's legends and traditions. We'll start at the sands of Dee.

1

THE SANDS OF DEE

Although Charles Kingsley was born in Devon, and lived there for much of his life, he came from an old Cheshire family, and between 1870 and 1873 he was Canon of Chester Cathedral. It was some years earlier, however, in 1850, that he wrote his most famous poem, 'The Sands of Dee', based on a tragic story from Wirral. It features in his first novel, *Alton Locke*, whose eponymous protagonist, a tailor, poet, and political radical, is present at a party where the heroine plays a plaintive air played on the piano. Then Alton hears

...two gentlemen, close to me, discuss a beautiful sketch by Copley Fielding, if I recollect rightly, which hung on the wall—a wild waste of tidal sands, with here and there a line of stake-nets fluttering in the wind—a grey shroud of rain sweeping up from the westward, through which low, red cliffs glowed dimly in the rays of the setting sun —a train of horses and cattle splashing slowly through shallow, desolate pools and creeks, their wet, red and black hides glittering in one long line of level light. One of the gentlemen had seen the spot represented, at the mouth of the Dee, and began telling wild stories of salmon-fishing and wild-fowl shooting—and then a tale of a girl, who, in bringing her father's cattle home across the sands, had been caught by a sudden flow of the tide upon the beach and was found next day a corpse hanging among the stake-nets far below. The tragedy, the art of the picture, the simple, dreary grandeur of the scenery, took possession of me, and I stood gazing a long time, and fancying myself pacing the sands. . . As I lay castle-building, Lillian's wild air still rang in my ears, and combined itself somehow with the picture of the Cheshire Sands, and the story of the drowned girl, till it shaped itself into a song...

I.

"O Mary, go and call the cattle home,
And call the cattle home,
And call the cattle home,
Across the sands o' Dee;"
The western wind was wild and dank wi' foam,
And all alone went she.

II.

The creeping tide came up along the sand,
And o'er and o'er the sand,
And round and round the sand,
As far as eye could see;
The blinding mist came down and hid the land -
And never home came she.

III.

"Oh, is it weed, or fish, or floating hair -
A tress o' golden hair,
Or drowned maiden's hair,
Above the nets at sea?
Was never salmon yet that shone so fair,
Among the stakes on Dee."

IV.

They rowed her in across the rolling foam,
The cruel crawling foam,
The cruel hungry foam,
To her grave beside the sea:
But still the boatmen hear her call the cattle home,
Across the sands o' Dee.

Wirral tradition locates the tale off the shore at Burton.

2
FROM CHESTER TO LITTLE STANNEY

We will here set in, at the tip of the toe, which comes to the Stone-bridge almost at Chester; and first, we will follow that water dividing this from Bolton hundred, which will bring us a little behind Upton to Chorlton, and then to the Lea, a fair house and fine desmesne, so called, and hath been the mansion for some descents of the Glaziers, esquires, of special note and good account. And next unto it lies Backford town and church, and hard by it the seat of our worthy promontory Henry Berkenhead, esquire, a gentleman whom the whole Country most deservedly acknowledges to have inherited, together with his place, that humanity and fair deportment that were in his fathers and ancestors before him.

From whence, as we go, we see on the west of us Capenhurst, a fine lordship, belonging to the houses of Cholmondeley and of Poole, and in the same one gentleman's seat.

By our brook lies Croughton, a member of the lordship of

John Hurleston, esquire; and from thence we come to Stoke, a little parish church adjoining to that lair desmesne and ancient seat of the Bunburies, of good worship, called Staney-hall, and which may be glad of the worthy present owner, Sir Henry Bunbury, knight, whose grave and well-disposed courses procure unto him a special good estimation for his endeavours to do good in public government, and his more private affairs also.

(William Webb)

The Headless Duck

Little Stanney, now best known for Cheshire Oaks Outlet Village, is also home to one of the strangest ghosts in England—the ghost of a duck. At one time, the people of Little Stanney were a laughing stock for miles around because they refused to go down the road to Stoak after nightfall. The reason, they said, was they were in danger of having their ankles pecked by a duck.

A group of villages led by the village butcher lay in wait for the duck and ambushed it. The butcher decapitated the creature with his trusty cleaver and buried its head in the ditch at the top of the lane. But even this did not solve the problem because from then on villagers were too afraid to use the lane since it was haunted by a headless duck.

They implored the parson to exorcise the ghost, but for all his efforts with bell, book and candle, the ghostly duck remained, to the terror of the villagers and the amusement of all for miles around.

3

NETHERPOOL

We turn us now towards our journey more westward, passing by Whitby; and from whence it may seem the Whitbys derived their name; of whom this gentleman that now bears part in the government of this city has advanced their names to no mean degree of deserved estimation.

Then holding our course we go by Great Sutton, a goodly lordship, and where hath been a famous seat called Sutton Court, the inheritance now of Sir Robert Cholmondely; and upon our other hand Pool, a fair ancient seat, with a park, of which the long-continued race of the Pools have borne that name, and it is very probable have been the ancestors of some very great families of that name in other counties; the present owner there John Pool, esquire. Near unto which we see also Stanlow, now a farm of the said Mr. Pool's.

The Pooles of Pool

Long ago, everyone's surname corresponded with
their trade, or was their nickname, or their father's
name, or the place they came from. The latter applied to
the Pooles of Pool, the local gentry of what is now
Netherpool and Overpool in the unromantic urban
sprawl of Ellesmere Port. Descendants of William de
Maldebeng, Baron of Nantwich, they owned land
throughout the Hundred of Wirral and the neighbouring
Broxton Hundred. The head of the family held the office
of Seneschal of Birkenhead Priory; and they were often
chosen as sheriffs, justiciaries or chamberlains of
Cheshire.

Others were bold knights and men-at-arms. Randall
de Poole fought in France during the Hundred Years'
War, in the van of the army under the Black Prince's
command, and also at Poitiers, under Lord Audley. Still
others inherited the reckless spirit of their warrior
forefathers, but turned their energies in other directions.

The annals of Liverpool record William, a younger
son of the Sir John Pool who was knighted in the days of
Richard II. It is believed that William, like many younger
sons from distinguished families, was involved in
privateering—piracy against enemy vessels in times of
war. But it seems sure that he was an out-and-out
criminal.

In 1436, "William Pulle of Wirral, gentleman, went to
Bewsey near Warrington with a great many servants,
and forcibly carried off Lady Isabel, widow of Sir John
Boteler, late constable of Liverpool Castle, and most
horribly ravished the said widow, carrying her into the
most desolate parts of Wales."

As we will see later, many of the gentry of medieval

Wirral were little more than bandits.

At another point, the Poole of the day married a Lady Ameline. Her husband gambled away the house and, the story goes, even his son and heir. She drowned their son in the lake of Poole Hall, and he shot her in retaliation. Ever since, Lady Ameline has haunted the hall, and workers employed there to this day are reluctant to visit certain areas.

The Pooles were staunch Catholics (like many of their peers), and had a priest's hole in the hall. In the Civil War, they became Cavaliers, and are said to have defended the house against Roundheads led by Sir William Moreton. The Roundheads were temporarily in control of the hall. Soldiers, possibly the same Roundheads, are said to have dragged the priest from his hole, and he 'died soon after.'

4

BRIMSTAGE

... there was a Monastery founded by the famous Lacy, constable of Chester, about the year 1173, taking the name from Staney-hill, but for the unruliness of the Mersey-Water they misliked their seat there, and found means to be translated from thence to Whaley, in Lancashire.

We come next to Hooton, a goodly ancient manor and fair park, which, ever since the reign of King Richard the Second, hath been the seat of the Stanleys of Hooton, gentlemen of great dignity and worth, deriving their pedigree from Allan Silvester, upon whom Ranulph the first Earl (of that name) of Chester bestowed the bailiwick of the forest of Wirral, and delivered unto him a horn, to be a token of his gift; from whence we gather that Wirral was holden to be a place of no mean account in those times; where have continued the same Stanleys in a direct succession, and was lately possessed by a very worthy and noble-minded knight, Sir Rowland Stanley, who lived there to the age, I have heard, of near one hundred years, and lived to be the oldest knight in this land; which I note the rather to approve the healthfulness of the place, and where his fourth generation, his son's son's son was at the time of his decease. Near unto which stands Eastham, the parish church and lordship.

Next beyond it we leave on our left hand Brinstone, (Brimstage)...

The Red Cat

The Red Cat is a popular pub name in Wirral, and throughout Cheshire. The existing pub in Greasby dates from 1964 (although it replaced an early establishment called the New Inn), but Brimstage was once home to an inn of the same name, whose license was revoked by the then Lord Leverhulme who demolished it in 1932 to make way for the village hall.

The village as a whole, and the surrounding land, is overlooked by Brimstage Hall, whose pele tower resembles those found on the Scottish Borders, but is unique in the Wirral area. When the tower was constructed is unknown, but the first reference to it comes from 1398, when Sir Hugh de Hulse and his wife Margery were granted a license to build an oratory, or chantry chapel, in Brimstage. The chapel still exists beneath the tower.

It is said that Lewis Carroll found inspiration in Brimstage. Son of a Cheshire parson, Charles Lutwidge Dodgson, (to give his real name), Oxford don, mathematician and pioneering photographer, is on record as visiting Brimstage. In his diary, he commented on how he "saw a Cheshire cat with a gigantic smile at Brimstage carved into the wall." This is believed to refer to a carved stone corbel in the shape of a cat's face in the so-called chapel. The phrase "Cheshire cat" and its association with smiling, predates the publication of *Alice in Wonderland* by many years.

It is maintained that there is a link between the name of the former inn, The Red Cat, and the legend of the grinning Cheshire cat. One theory says that the Red Cat was the badge of the Barons of Montalt (Mold), one of the noble families of medieval Cheshire. Lady Margery was a Domville, and this family is believed to be a junior branch of the Montalt family. Originally intended to represent a red lion, the badge looked more like a grinning red cat; hence the pub name and hence the Cheshire cat. And, in Wirral at least, it is said to be the Cheshire cat in Brimstage that inspired the cat who appears in the works of Lewis Carroll.

Sir John Troutbeck and the Battle of Blore Heath

Sir Hugh and Margery had a son, whose only child was a daughter. In 1440, she married Sir John Troutbeck, Lord of Dunham-on-the-Hill and Chamberlain of Chester, who became, by this marriage, lord of Little Neston, Oxton, Raby, Barnston, and of course Brimstage. This was at the beginning of the Wars of the Roses, and three years after his wife's death, Sir John joined the Lancastrians, under Queen Margaret of Anjou, the "she-wolf of France." He was slain at the Battle of Blore Heath.

The old chronicle of Hall says of this battle that over two thousand people were killed: "…But the greatest plague lighted on the Cheshire men, because one half of the shire was on the one part, and the other on the other part …"

Drayton, describing the battle in in his *Polyolbion*, refers to all the great families of medieval Cheshire, including the Troutbecks:

> *There Dutton Dutton kills, a Done doth kill a Done;*
> *A Booth a Booth, and Leigh by Leigh is overthrown;*
> *A Venables against a Venables doth stand,*
> *And Troutbeck fighteth with a Troutbeck hand to hand.*
> *There Molineux doth make a Molineux to die,*
> *And Egerton the strength of Egerton doth try.*
> *O Cheshire, wert thou mad! of thine own native gore,*
> *So much until this day thou never shed'st before.*
> *Above two thousand men upon the earth were thrown*
> *Of which the greatest part were naturally thine own.*

5

POULTON LANCELYN

…and so come to Pooton, or Poulton, of which name there is another township, from which this is distinguished by the name of Lancelot…

Poulton Lancelot

According to tradition, Lancelot lived at Poulton Lancelyn, and it is named after him. Lord Byron added a note to his poem *Francesca Da Rimini*, explaining a reference to the Arthurian knight Sir Lancelot as follows:

"One of the Knights of Arthur's Round Table, and the lover of Genevra (i.e. *Queen Guinevere*), celebrated in romance… Whitaker, the historian of Manchester, makes out for the knight both 'a local habitation and a name.' 'The name of Lancelot,' he says 'is an appellative truly British and significative of royalty; lance being a celtic word for spear, and *leod, lod,* or *lot* importing a people.

He was therefore a British Sovereign, and since he is denominated Lancelot of the lake, perhaps! he ... was king of Cheshire, and resided at Pool-ton Lancelot, in the Hundred of Wirrall..."

Ghosts of Poulton Hall

Nathaniel Hawthorne, who lived nearby in Rock Ferry when he was American consul, recorded a legend connected with Poulton Hall concerning 'an attic chamber, with a skylight, called the "martyr's chamber," from having in olden times been tenanted by a lady who was imprisoned there, and persecuted to death for religion...'

There was also a locked room in the hall that remained unopened for half a century. One of the Greene family shot himself while in the room, and his ghost was said to haunt it. When it was reopened in 1910, a panelled room was discovered, with a library of four thousand books collected by Reverend Thomas Greene, Rector of Woodchurch in the early eighteenth century.

Another legend associated with Poulton Hall is that of the phantom hitchhiker, or ghostly nun, who haunts the bridge across the Dibbin on the road from Bromborough to Spital, and other roads in the vicinity. In 1970, a woman on her way back from Clatterbridge Hospital saw a girl waiting for a lift by the side of the road, but as the woman approached, the girl vanished. In the same year she was seen again by a motorist. Later, a man driving along Poulton Road stopped to offer a lift to a woman in a long dark coat, but as he opened his door she vanished.

It is said to be the ghost of a girl who left Poulton

Hall to go to a nunnery. As she crossed the bridge, she was attacked by a man who raped her and then murdered her before flinging her body into the stream below. An alternative version of the story says that the nun was walking from Birkenhead Priory to St. Werburgh's Abbey in Chester when she spent the night in a manor house near the bridge. The lord of the manor is said to have starved her to death because she refused his advances.

In yet another version he beheaded her, and in some stories the ghost is a headless nun.

6
BROMBOROUGH

…and the next to that is Brumbrough, a pretty town, with a chapel; and therein Daniel Bavand, esquire, hath a fair house and desmesne…

The Battle of Brunanburh

Local folklore says that the crucial battle of Brunanburh, fought in 937 between Saxons and Vikings for control of England, was fought near Bromborough. Certainly, a battle of some sort seems to have left its mark on the surrounding landscape. Red Hill Road in Bebington is said to be named after the hill on which the blood of slaughtered men ran down. Nearby is Soldiers' Hill, also said to commemorate the events of the fight, as well as the so-called 'Battlefields.' It is also said that Kings Road in Bebington is named after the king who fought nearby, with a note to the effect that it has not been improved since that day. Near Bromborough itself lie the War Graves, where it is believed the slain warriors were buried. But what caused the battle? Although contemporary accounts are sparse, later traditions from Wirral and beyond tell the following story:

Athelstan, king of Wessex, made peace with the Viking king of York, Sihtric, married his sister to him and sponsored his baptism. Not long after Athelstan had returned home, Sihtric thought better of his decision, and threw out his new wife and his new religion at the same time. In response, Athelstan marched into Sihtric's kingdom and conquered it, and Sihtric was forced to flee to his relatives in Dublin. Shortly after, he died and he was succeeded by his nephew Anlaf.

Anlaf was not content with ruling Dublin and he decided to win back the kingdom of York. He hatched a plot with Constantinus, king o' Scots, and the Cumbrian king, Owen, to attack Athelstan's realm. Sailing from Dublin, he met the Scots off the Isle of Man, then sailed along the Cumbrian coast to pick up their other allies. It seems that Anlaf also had support from the Norsemen who had settled in Wirral. According to local legend, his entire army landed at Bromborough Pool, from which they intended to march into Athelstan's lands and lay them waste.

Athelstan had received word of the plot and he mustered his own forces, sending word to Anlaf that he would meet him to fight a battle on a particular day. The field he chose for the battle lay in the vicinity of Brunanburh, now Bromborough. On the chosen day, the battle lines were drawn with Anlaf and his armies near Bromborough Court House and Athelstan's armies on Bebington Heath.

Seeing what danger faced him, Anlaf conceived a plan. He put aside his royal regalia and dressed himself as a minstrel, taking a harp and making his way undetected through the Saxon lines to the tent of King Athelstan. Here he stood singing and strumming his harp, and he was soon allowed into the tent to entertain the king and his men, who were feasting. As he sang, his eyes were everywhere, examining everything he could see in the tent.

When the king and his men finished eating, Anlaf received gold and was ordered to depart. He left the tent, but disdaining such payment, he buried the gold in the ground. He was seen doing this by the king's chancellor Thorketil, a man who had once been Anlaf's warrior but now fought for Athelstan. Entering the king's tent, Thorketil told him what he had seen.

The king cursed him for not recognising their enemy when he stood before the king, but Thorketil said, "The same oath which I have lately sworn to you, O king, I formerly made to Anlaf: and had you seen me violate it towards him, you might have expected that I would have been guilty of similar perfidy towards yourself. But listen to the advice of your servant; remaining in another place till the rest of the army come up, you will destroy your ferocious enemy by a moderate delay."

The king approved of this, and at once he gave the order to strike camp and move to another spot. So they camped along the ridge that now runs from Spital to Higher Bebington.

Anlaf returned to his men after his spying mission and ordered a night attack. He led his men forward to find the new camp of the king, where a bishop had joined the army with all his men. Anlaf's warriors slew him, then they marched on to find Athelstan unprepared and asleep, despite the forewarning he had received, because he had not expected a night attack.

When the noise of battle roused him, he urged his people to join the fight, whereupon by chance his sword fell from the sheath. Everyone was filled with fear, but Athelstan called upon God and Saint Aldhelm to protect them and put his hand on the scabbard again to find the sword still there.

Heartened by this miracle, and by the first lights of dawn in the east, Athelstan led his forces against Anlaf's troops, while Thorketil led the men of London and the Midlands against the Scots and Cumbrians. After a few volleys of arrows and shot, the battle was fought on foot, and many men were slain.

They fought for a long time with great courage, and neither side would give ground. It was close to sunset when Thorketil took with him some Londoners noted for their valour and a man from Hereford called Singin, who was taller and brawnier than the others. They charged at the head of their men and broke through the ranks, striking Scots down on either side. With arrows sticking out of his armour so he resembled a hedgehog, Thorketil led his men deep into the masses of Scots and Cumbrians. Finally he reached the son of King Constantinus himself, dragged him from his horse, and tried to take him prisoner. The Scots crowded round, attempting to rescue their prince, and set upon Thorketil who was beginning to repent his rashness.

But at that moment, Singin stabbed the prince and slew him. When news of his son's death reached him, Constantinus took to flight, and all his men followed him.

To quote Tennyson's translation of a contemporary poem:

Constantinus,
 Crept to his north again,
Hoar-headed hero!
 Slender warrant had
 he to be proud of
The welcome of war-knives
He that was reft of his
Folk and friends that had
Fallen in conflict
Leaving his son too
Lost in the carnage,
 Mangled to morsels,
 A youngster in war!
 Slender reason had
 He to be glad of
The clash of the war-glaive —
 Traitor and trickster
 And spurner of treaties —
He nor had Anlaf
 With armies so broken
A reason for bragging
That they had the better
 In perils of battle
 On places of slaughter —
 The struggle of standards
The rush of the javelins
The crash of the charges
The wielding of weapons —
The play that they play'd with
 The children of Edward.
Then with their nailed prows
Parted the Norsemen, a
Blood-reddened relic of

Javelins over
The jarring breaker, the deep-sea billow,
Shaping their way toward Dyflen[1] again,
Shamed in their souls.

Also the brethren,
King and Atheling,
Each in his glory,
Went to his own in his own West-Saxonland,
Glad of the war.

Many a carcase they left to be carrion,
Many a livid one, many a sallow-skin —
Left for the white-tailed eagle to tear it, and
Left for the horny-tailed raven to rend it, and
Gave to the garbaging war-hawk to gorge it, and
That grey beast, the wolf of the weald.

Never had huger
Slaughter of heroes
Slain by the sword-edge —
Such as old writers
Have writ of in histories —
Hapt in this isle, since
Up from the East hither
Saxon and Angle from
Over the broad billow
Broke into Britain with
Haughty war-workers who
Harried the Welshman, when
Earls that were lured by the
Hunger of glory gat
Hold of the land.

---

[1] *Dublin.*

The Vikings are said to have fled from the Dee shore, and ever was the Mersey a river of ill omen to them.

Wells of Bromborough

Bromborough once had several famous wells. St. Patrick's Well is still to be found in Brotherton Park. It is said to have been blessed by St. Patrick when he came ashore in AD 432, and here he baptised his converts. He is also said to have gone on to preach in what is now Standish Street in Liverpool before setting off on his first trip to Ireland.

St. Chad, who converted the whole area to Christianity in the seventh century, (following a lapse caused by the Anglo Saxon invasions), had a well of his own. It was to be found in Shodwell Wood, until it was destroyed during the building of the now-demolished power station.

Third was the Petrifying Well, near the Otters' Tunnel that leads under the Chester railway line. It is thought to have had links with the old leper hospital at Spital, founded by the Lancelyn family in the Middle Ages. Writing in the fifties, Norman Ellison explained the name was because this "heavily impregnated spring" coated anything placed in it with a stone-like substance.

Sadly, the well seems to have since transformed itself into a muddy puddle on the hillside.

7
BEBINGTON

…next which lies Nether Bebbington and Over Bebbington, the precincts whereof take up in this tract a large extent; the one a church town with a fair church and goodly parsonage, the other a member of the parish where John Minshal, esquire, of Minshall, hath great store of fair possessions.

Bebington Church

St. Andrews, parish church of Bebington, is the linchpin of numerous stories. Robert Nixon[2], the so-called 'Palatine Prophet' who lived in the days of Richard III and Henry VII[3], foretold that when the ivy reaches the top of the church spire, the world will come to an end. The good folk of Wirral needed not be too disheartened, however, since Nixon also told a man who he met in Storeton Woods that in the last days the one

---

[2] *Nixon is said to have been "a short squab fellow, had a great head and goggle eyes, that he used to drivel as he spoke, which was very seldom, and was extremely surly... Against Children he particularly had a spite, especially if they made any sport of him, and would run after them and beat them. At first he was a plough boy to Farmer Crowton of Swanton, and so stubborn, they could make him do nothing without beating. They could seldom get any thing out of him but Yes and No, unless he was pinched with hunger; for he had a very good stomach, and could eat up a shoulder of mutton at one meal, with a good hunch of bread and cheese after it..." His first prophecy occurred when he was ploughing. He stopped his work and was heard to say 'Now Dick. Now Harry. Now Dick, Now Harry,' several times. In the end it transpired that he was witnessing the events of the Battle of Bosworth Field, many miles away, where Richard III (Dick) was defeated by Henry Tudor, later Henry VII. Many other prophecies followed, until his fame as a prophet reached the ears of the king, who "would needs see this fool; [Nixon] cried, and made much ado that he might not go to court, and the reason he gave was that he should be starved. The King being informed of Nixon's refusing to come, said he would take particular care that he should not be starved; and ordered him to be brought up... That Nixon might be well provided for, it was ordered he should be kept in the kitchen; but he grew so troublesome in licking and picking the meat, that the cooks locked him up in a hole, and the King going on a sudden from Hampton Court to London, they forgot Nixon in the hurry, and he was starved to death."*

[3] *Or James I, according to other accounts.*

safe place to be would be "God's croft, between the rivers Mersey and Dee."

Despite this divine protection, the spire was struck by lightning in 1805, and it was rebuilt after further storm damage. Finally, the ivy was grubbed out in 1911, due to the damage it had done to the spire. Today, the lack of ivy on the spire is conspicuous. What effect this will have on the future of the world is something about which we can only speculate.

Nineteenth century Cheshire poet Egerton Leigh wrote the following lines concerning the spire and its ivy.

I.

IVY! thou art fresh and young,
Gleaming in the morning sun:
In thee change is never seen,
Through the year an evergreen.

II.

When at banquet held on high,
The maid Kissos merrily
Danced, and Bacchus oft embraced,
As midst gods she wanton raced.

III.

Whilst she frolicked up and down,
Down she sank upon the ground;
Exhausted, closed her eyes in death.
Panting fled her fluttering breath.

IV.

Ivy sprang up round the maid.
By the Greeks hence named ('tis said)

Kissos which the oak entwines.
As Kissos once, the god of wines.

V.

Ivy, though so bright and green,
Oft near death is met, I ween;
Midst the' old castle's ruins creeps,
From winding-sheet of snow-wreath peeps,

VI.

Throws its tendrils round the oak,
Which its fond embraces choke;
Like the snake-encircling coils,
Whelming hapless prey in toils.

VII.

Ivy twined with gloomy yew,
Too oft meets the mourner's view;
Slowly following the dead
To their last cold churchyard bed.

VIII.

Hast thou heard what hast been said
By seer Nixon, prophet dread?
Of Bebington's high-soaring spire
Thus he spoke in words of fire:

Nixon's prophecy.

IX.

When that spire's vane shall clasp
Ivy with its fatal grasp,
Then the last stern trumpet's call
Live and dead shall summon all,

X.

Then shall hap the crash of doom;
Then the dead shall burst the tomb;
Together crushed the world shall roll,
Like a parched, flame-shrivelled scroll!'

XI.

Many years since then have passed,
Still the world and spire last;
Nor yet th' ivy's fatal grasp
Dares the fatal point to clasp.

XII.

Once it almost reached the height,
Filling Cheshire with affright;
When the lightning's scorching blast,
Through the threatening ivy past.

XIII.

Twice since then in utmost need,
Chance hath baulked the ivy's greed;
Still the tendrils seek the sky.
Struggling towards the spire on high.

MORAL.

XIV.

May our hearts to heaven rise.
Then we ne'er shall fear surprise;
E'en should th' ivy top the spire.
And the doomed world wrap in fire.

Among the yews in the churchyard, near the family vault of the Lancelyn Greens, stands a lamppost said to have inspired the one that appears in CS Lewis' *The Lion, the Witch and the Wardrobe*. Roger Lancelyn Green was a friend of CS Lewis, and JRR Tolkien too, and both were regular visitors to Poulton Hall.

The church is said to have been constructed on top of a burial mound, possibly a centre of pagan worship. This explains the dangerous bend in Church Road, which follows the line of the mound. The circular shape supposedly relates to a pagan belief that evil spirits could hide in corners.

According to legend, the church was originally intended to be built at Tranmere, but one morning the builders found that all the materials had been moved to their present location by "some unnamed force." The sturdy workmen continued building in this new location. A similar story is told about the church at Stoak, and also the church at Over near Delamere. In both of these cases the church was moved by the Devil himself.

In the early days of Christianity in Wirral, St Andrews was known as Whitchurch, or the White Church, due to the creamy Storeton sandstone from which it was built. Bones and swords and spearheads were found beneath the church in the nineteenth century, and it is believed that they were the remains of warriors who died at the battle of Brunanburh (937 AD), fought in the vicinity, according to some stories (see the chapter on Bromborough above). At night, ghostly monks have been seen, some floating above the level of the ground, others seemingly wading through the earth.

The Wishing Gate

There was once a farm gate on the corner where

Bracken Lane and Red Hill Road meet Mount Road. A normal wooden field-gate with every surface covered by initials and dates, it was known as the Wishing Gate.

The custom was that couples would stop here, hold hands through the bars of the gate to make a wish and plight their troth. It even became the subject of a poem by local poet John Foster Pride: "The Wishing Gate at Bebington." It is now the location of Wishing Gate Cottage.

The King's Breeches

An old saying had it that "the king's breeches bought the Rock Ferry." The story goes that the Prince Regent, later George IV, was one of the many aristocrats who hunted with hounds in Cheshire. One hunt meet, he noticed the cut of the Marquis of Cholmondely's buckskin breeches, and liking what he saw, Prinny (as he was popularly known) asked the Marquis the name of his tailor.

"John White, of Nantwich,' the Marquis replied.

"Then he shall make me a pair," the Prince Regent declared.

The tailor of Nantwich received the Prince Regent's order, and as a result White became the most sought-after tailor amongst huntsmen and sportsmen.

He moved to London and made a vast fortune, some of which he invested in the ferry that gave its name to Rock Ferry, which he later sold to a Mr. Morecroft, who built the Rock Slip for £20, 000, and may be regarded as the founder of Rock Ferry itself.

8 STORETON

Upon our left hand we leave Stoorton, a lordship...

The Story of the Wirral Horn

Today the Wirral Horn is used to represent the Borough of Wirral, but in its day, according to local historian Paul Booth, it was a symbol of repression. Indeed, many of the men who bore it led bands of rapacious cutthroats and thieves, so it is perhaps ironic that it should now be used as the badge of the local authority.

After the Norman Conquest, the people of Wirral rose in rebellion against the invaders, raiding the neighbourhood of Chester, according to some traditions in league with the Welsh. As a punishment, in 1120 the Hundred of Wirral was turned into a royal forest. This did not mean that it was heavily wooded (*Domesday Book* only records substantial woodland in Prenton), or that the populace was deported, as some traditions claim; it was a hunting preserve for the use of the king, and the inhabitants were subject to the harsh and repressive forest laws introduced into England by William the Conqueror himself, who set aside whole areas of the country as forests.

Forest law forbade the enclosure of pastures, clearing land for farming, or felling trees or shrubs. The inhabitants were also not permitted to carry hunting weapons, and dogs were banned, except for mastiffs. The latter were were allowed as watchdogs, but their front claws had to be removed to stop them hunting the king's game.

The most famous medieval forest was of course Sherwood, famous in legend for its outlaws. Wirral also became a haunt of nefarious persons, as the anonymous author of the fourteenth century poem Sir Gawayne and the Grene Knight made clear:

> ...All the isles of Anglesey on his left hand he holds,
> and fares over the fords by the forelands
> over at the Holy Head, till he regained the shore
> in the wilderness of Wirral—lived there few
> who either God or man with good heart loved.

According to the inscription on the Wirral Horn, which is now in the possession of the Earl of Cromer: In the year 1120 Randal de Meschines, Earl of Chester, created Alan Sylvester chief forester of the forest of Wirral, and granted to him the manors of Hooten, Storeton and Puddington to hold upon the condition that he performed the duties of forester, and in addition that he blew or caused to be blown a horn at the Gloverstone in Chester on the morning of every fair day, to indicate that the tolls on all goods bought or sold in the city or within sound of that horn belonged to the Earl or his tenants. Alan Sylvester was succeeded by his son Ralph, on whose death, without issue, Hugh Cyvelioc, Earl of Chester, granted the same manors with the forester-ship to Alexander de Storeton on his marriage with Annabella, the daughter of Alan Sylvester. Alexander de Storeton again had only female issue, and the forestership passed next to Sir Thomas Bamville, who married Agnes de Storeton, daughter of Alexander. Sir Philip Bamville, the heir of Sir Thomas, also left issue, three daughters only, the eldest of whom, Jane, married Sir William de Stanley, and brought the forestership as part of her dower, the title of her son, John Stanley, having been proved in 1346 before Jordan de Macclesfield, Justice in Eyre to the Earl of Chester. In this family it remained until disafforested by King Edward III on the complaints of the citizens of Chester, who represented that they were grievous sufferers from the freebooters who lurked in the forest. The Stanleys petitioned the King for remuneration for the loss of the profits attached to the office of chief forester, and were granted an annuity of twenty marks, which, however, seems to have been but indifferently paid ...

The Stanleys

The marriage of William de Stanley and Jane (or Joan) de Storeton, by which the Stanley family became master foresters of Wirral, is recorded in detail:

... on Sunday after the feast of St Mathew the Apostle and Evangelist... on the 27th Sept 1282, Philip de Bamville, with his wife and family, was at a banquet given by Master John de

Stanley (a priest), on which occasion Jane, suspecting that her father intended to marry her to her step-mother's son, took means to avoid it by repairing with William de Stanley to Astbury Church, where they uttered the following mutual promise, he saying, 'Jane, I plight thee my troth to take and hold thee as my lawful wife until my life's end,' and she replying, 'I, Jane, take thee, William, as my lawful husband.' The witnesses were Adam de Hoton and Dawe de Copeland...

William and Joan had a son, also called William, who became master forester after his father. Little is recorded of this William, except that he asserted "The right of the bailiwick of the Forest of Wirral and the Manor of Storeton," and he had two sons, the elder also named William, the younger called John.

The third Sir William Stanley inherited the forestership and the manor of Storeton, or rather, a third of the latter, since the descendants of Jane de Storeton's sisters held the other two thirds.

The Black Prince

In 1353 the Black Prince visited Chester. He ordered a forest court to be convened, during which a series crimes were laid at the door of the master forester and his men. The court found Sir William Stanley guilty of extracting money from townships for allowing them to keep their sheep in the woods at fawning time, of taking bribes from a former prior of Birkenhead to allow assarting (clearing waste land for farming) in the forest and impressing labour from several villages to work in his fields during harvest time.

Forester John Laselles was found guilty of crimes in Wallasey: he stole a boat at Seacombe, assaulted a man at Liscard and tied him to a post, forced the servant of local squire Henry Litherland to enter his service and assaulted another man at Poulton by shooting arrows at him. The same court claimed that Wirral foresters terrorised Wirral people and issued threats so they would not make complaints. John Domville of Brimstage and Richard Hough of Thornton were accused of illegally hunting in the forest and leading criminal raids across the Mersey. In defence they claimed the Earl of Chester (the Black Prince himself, or perhaps his predecessor) pardoned them of all "burglaries, prison-breaking, rapes, poisonings and conspiracies." The court was eventually cancelled and a cash payment of 5000 marks extracted.

This fine was precisely what the Black Prince wanted: he was planning a campaign against the French and money was in short supply. Wirral dissatisfied him since there were few archers in the Hundred, which is unsurprising since owning hunting bows was forbidden under forest law. Despite this, and despite the accusations against him, Sir William Stanley and his merry men joined the Black Prince in the war against the French. The campaign was to end at the Battle of Poitiers, where the French were defeated and their king, John the Good, was taken prisoner.

But Sir William Stanley was not present at this famous victory. During the campaign, he murdered a man named Richard de Becheton. The king's officers arrested him for his crime and he had the forestership of Wirral confiscated. Once the war was over, however, he was released, reinstated and compensated for loss of revenue.

Some years later, Sir William Stanley acquired a third of Storeton manor, which had previously belonging to the Becheton family. His grandfather's marriage with Jane de Storeton had only yielded a third of the estate; the two other thirds had gone to the husbands of Jane's sisters, and Richard de Becheton was descended from one of them. It seems that Sir William had his eye on the whole estate. By murdering Richard, he went some way to securing two thirds of the manor.

Sir William and Sir John his brother next became involved in the territorial disputes of the Vernon family, Barons of Shipbrook. This is covered in more detail in the chapter on Thurstaston.

The End of the Forest

In 1376 the Black Prince died. In the same year there was the Petition of the "poor Commonalty of Wyrall" who "had suffered great harm, damage, and destruction" from the beasts of the forest, so that even the Churches were desolate and divine services were withheld. Wirral was disafforested by Edward III, although deer parks remained at Shotwick, Puddington, Neston, Hooton, and Bidston.

Although there is no sign of Neston deer park, its gates are remembered in the place-name Parkgate. The wall that surrounded Bidston deer park is still to be seen on Bidston Hill, and is known as the 'Penny-a-day dyke,' since the workers who built it were supposedly paid a penny a day.

The same year, William's brother John, and Henry Harper of Wervin, were outlawed for murdering Thomas Clotton. Clotton had married the daughter of William Laken and acquired the last third of Storeton estate. John Stanley and Harper were eventually pardoned at the behest of Sir Thomas Trivet. After this point Sir William Stanley acquired the last third of Storeton estate, which had belonged to the Laken family.

Sir William Stanley's post as Master Forester was abolished, along with the Forest of Wirral itself. But John, who had quietly aided William in all his "burglaries, prison-breaking, rapes, poisonings and conspiracies" and had been outlawed for murdering one of his brother's enemies, found his fortunes growing by the day.

Virtue Rewarded

After marrying the heiress of Lathom in Lancashire (despite the disapproval of John of Gaunt), John Stanley went from strength to strength. Having the good sense to support Henry IV at the Battle of Shrewsbury, John was greatly favoured, being made Lord Lieutenant of Ireland, King of the Isle of Man and Knight of the Garter. Distinguishing himself again in Ireland, John died there, and his remains were interred at Burscough Abbey near Ormskirk.

Finally, in return for a pivotal act of treachery against Richard III, Henry VII conferred upon John's grandson Thomas the title "Earl of Derby," which has remained in his family until the present day.

9 PRENTON

…and so go by Prenton, where one race of the Hawkenhals have a fine house and desmesne; the present owner thereof John Hokenhall, esquire.

Prenton Hall

In the old Wirral dialect, ghosts were known as "buggens", a word of Welsh origin related to *bogle* and *bugbear*. There was a rhyme about the buggen of Prenton Hall:

When gorse is in blossom and holly is green,
Prenton Hall buggen is then to be seen.

It is not on record what the buggen looks like, although in 1961 a visitor to the Hall saw the ghost of a monk watching her in the lounge. Prenton Hall was once a grange (farm) belonging to Birkenhead Priory, so perhaps the buggen is a monastic spirit.

At one point, probably in the nineteenth century, an old lady lived at the Hall with her maid. The maid was working downstairs one day when she heard from upstairs what sounded like a cascade of coins. Thinking her mistress had dropped money in the room above, she hurried up the staircase to help her. The old lady had also heard the noise, and she was on her way down to see what had happened when the maid met her on the stairs.

It appears that at some point a bag of money had been hidden in the wall, and over the years the bag rotted away until the money fell that day. No one knows who put it there, or why, but perhaps it was a gift from the Prenton Hall buggen!

The Prenton Doll's House

According to urban legend, a doll's house once stood in a front garden in Prenton; an exact replica of the main house, a three-bedroomed semi. It was made out of bricks and was quite large—like a Wendy house. It had been built as a memorial to the young daughter of the couple who lived there, after she was killed by a hit-and-run driver while playing in the street.

Inside it was a doll dressed in a replica of the clothes worn by the girl on the day when she had been killed. According to the story, the doll itself had a wig made from the girl's hair, and even included her teeth in its mouth. The doll sat in the house staring out at the road through the front window. It remained there for many years, becoming the focus of disturbing legends, until the council demolished the whole street. Garages now stand on the site.

10
LANDICAN AND WOODCHURCH

Beyond which lieth Lanian, or Llandecan, a township with pretty farms in it, the lands of Sir Richard Wilbraham, knight and baronet; and from thence we go next to Woodchurch, a parish church and a neat parsonage by it;

Landican as a place name is believed to be Welsh in origin, the *llan* (enclosure, or more specifically, church) of Tegan, an early Celtic saint. Although today it is most notable for the large municipal cemetery, the village does not have a church, and is in the parish of Woodchurch. It is believed, however, that the parish church now dedicated to Holy Cross was once the church of Saint Tegan. It is not unusual for churches to have been built at some distance from a village, and numerous stories have been told to explain this, such as those mentioned in the chapter on Bebington.

No such story is told of Woodchurch, but like St

Andrews in Bebington and the lost church at Overchurch, Holy Cross lies in a circular enclosure. This is thought to represent the Celtic 'llan', and to predate the adoption of the site by Christianity. It is widely believed, in fact, that the site was originally a centre of Druidic worship—hence the nearby road 'Druids Way,'—and that the wood of which the original church was clearly built came from the trees of a pre-existing Druidic grove. Another nearby road name, Pool Lane, refers to a pool now drained that was to be seen in the churchyard up until the mid-twentieth century. A small bronze cauldron and spearhead were found here, and it has been speculated that they were votive offerings from Druidic times.

The Welsh name for Wirral, *Cilgwri*, usually translated as 'The Corner', has also been translated as 'Gwri's enclosure.' Gwri was the childhood name of the legendary hero Pryderi. One of Pryderi's adventures was to accompany the High King Bran the Blessed in his war against Ireland, during which the Cauldron of Rebirth—a precursor to the Holy Grail—was seized as booty. It has been suggested that on returning to Britain, Pryderi took refuge in Cilgwri (Wirral). Perhaps he brought with him the Cauldron. Since the Cauldron is the prototype for the Holy Grail, could that mean that Holy Cross is in fact the Grail Chapel of legend? But we will see that Woodchurch is not the only place in Wirral with Grail-associations.

Woodchurch's mystical and mythical connections are at the heart of the *Cauldron Series* written by novelist and filmmaker Tom Stevens.

11

BIRKENHEAD

... looking towards the Mersey again, lies a goodly vale and pleasant track in which we may see Upton, a fine lordship, wherein stand the house and desmesne, where a long descent of gentlemen have had continuance, sprung from the house of Bould, of Bould in Lancashire, the now owner thereof Peter Bould, esquire, to whom I owe particular respects of love and next unto this Oxton; and then nearer to the Mersey side the township of Tranmore; and near to that is a fine seat of that worthy gentleman, whom elsewhere we remembered, John Minshal, of Minshal, esquire, called Derby House.

Thence, on our left hand, we see Caughton — [Claughton] where Mr. Thomas Powell hath fair lands; and then leaving the ferry, where the passage lies over into Lancashire, to Liverpool, we step over into Berket-wood [Birkenhead], and where hath been a famous priory, the foundation whereof I am not yet instructed for, but now a very goodly desmesne, and which is become (by descent from the Worsleys, men of great possessions) now to a gentleman of much worth, Thomas Powell, esquire, the heir of that ancient seat of Horsley, in the county of Flint, and one whom our county may gladly receive to be added to the number of those that deserve better commendation than I am fit to give them; though unto him I am particularly bound to extend my wits to a higher reach than here I will make trial of.

The Treasure of Birkenhead Priory

Birkenhead Priory now stands in the middle of an industrial estate near Cammell Lairds shipyard. It was founded by Hamon de Massie, third Baron of Dunham Massey, in the mid-twelfth century, for sixteen monks of the Benedictine Order. As well as being landowners, the monks operated a ferry across the Mersey, the nearby Monks Ferry, and like many priories and abbeys Birkenhead Priory grew very rich. Legend says that beneath the Priory were several tunnels, one running to the later site of Mother Redcap's in Wallasey, and another stretching under the river to Liverpool.

In 1318, Edward II visited Birkenhead where he granted the Prior the right to erect a hostelry for the many travellers passing through from North Wales to Ireland, via Liverpool, and pilgrims going to Our Lady of Hilbre.

In 1538 Henry VIII carried out the Dissolution of the Monasteries, in which his men closed down the monasteries and claimed their property for the crown. According to legend, when the king's men came to Birkenhead Priory, a monk fled into the tunnels, carrying with him the Priory's treasure. The tunnel entrance collapsed behind him, and it has never been found again, but monks' ghosts are said to haunt the area still.

The Old Priory (Before Renovated) by WW Townshend

Gaunt and grim the Priory stands
Dust-stained with age, and grey;
Ivy bedecks the eaves and walls
Fast crumbling to decay.
O'er moss-clad fallen stones the weeds
Entwined with prickly briar –
'A roofless wreck' o'ershadowed by
St. Mary's towering spire.

Yet long ago, thou, too, wast grand,
Noble, and fair to see,
The Mersey 'neath thy sacred walls
Paid homage unto thee;
Kissing the daisied and primrose banks
With the swirl of a swelling tide;
Where seabirds undisturbed would hie,
On the flowing stream to ride.

From stately trees the thrush piped high
A matin and evensong,
The squirrel perched on the highest branch
Free and far from the madding throng;
And holy monks, with solemn tread,
Would wend their way to prayer,
In answer to the vesper bell,
For peace, sweet peace! reigned there.

But ah! how strange the scene today –
Marked is the change, I trow,
For monk, and cowl, and vesper bell
Are vanished long ago.
Where once was solitude and calm,

There is now a city's din,
Vale, wood, and bell have disappeared,
King Commerce has stept in.

But sweet romance still clings to thee,
Though robbed of pomp and state
In the ancient days of civil strife,
When Cromwell sealed thy fate.

Gaunt and grim the Priory stands
Silent in its vesper chimes,
Dust-stained with age, a crumbling wreck,
A relic of olden times.

The Green Lane Ghost Train

In 1971, a man living near the Old Chester Road heard a noise from the railway at about one in the morning. Looking out of his window he saw a steam train travelling down the line from Green Lane station towards Bebington. This sighting was a rarity, but the Green Lane ghost train had been heard numerous times, particularly in the early years of the twenty first century.

Writing on the *North-East Wales* website, Neil Hayden reported that his father, who worked on the trains long ago, had heard it frequently, the sound of a passing steam train long after the track had been electrified, in the early hours of the morning when no trains were running.

Customs and Traditions

In nineteenth century Birkenhead, on Easter Monday, children would gather in the Park carrying baskets of coloured eggs. The child who had the biggest and most colourful eggs won a prize, and then the children played a game with the eggs, rolling them down the grassy mounds near Ashville Road, known locally as the Bonks. Wickets were placed at the foot of the mounds, and the object of the game was to roll the eggs through these wickets without breaking them. The two best players were given prizes and afterwards some of the children performed an Easter Egg Dance.

The Bonks, which may have been prehistoric burial mounds, were later declared to be an eyesore by the town council, who had them demolished.

In the 1840s May Day was celebrated with a carnival, during which a procession went from Abbey Street, down from Chester Street, up Hamilton Street and to a green field, site of the later Hinson Street, where the Maypole was erected and a collection was taken. The procession was made up of men dressed as women, wearing bright chintz dresses, including a male May Queen, sometimes bearded! When the procession reached the field, women joined the group and together they danced around the Maypole.

Later, the parade consisted of lorries containing tableaux, bands, and dancers, with the fire engine at the back. This came to an end with the First World War, although, according to Norman 'Nomad' Ellison, as late as the fifties a "pathetic relic" could be seen in the poorer areas of Birkenhead, where children escorted a May Queen and asked for pennies, which Nomad regarded as a degeneration into "shameless cadging."

In Oxton and Claughton in the nineteenth century, the Mummers play was performed at Christmas by mummers known as the Golloshons. These seem to have been connected with the Mummers' carvings on Bidston Hill. The last performance was in 1935.

12
WALLASEY

Beyond which, we have only that other Poulton called by the name of Seacombe, till we come to the north-western shore, laying upon the Vergivian or Irish Sea, where are situate the township, parish and church of Kirby, in Walley, or Walsey, a town which hath fair lands, and where lie those fair sands, or plains, upon the shore of the sea, which, for the fitness for such a purpose, allure the gentlemen and others oft to appoint great matches and venture no small sums in trying the swiftness of their horses.

The Building of St. Hilary's

St Hilary's, the parish church in Wallasey Village, is dedicated to St Hilary of Poitiers, a bishop of Poitiers in the mid fourth century AD. It is believed that the church owes its dedication to another Gaulish saint, Germanus (St Germain), bishop of Auxerre in the following century, who came to Britain to combat the Pelagian heresy, a belief that salvation could be attained by works rather than grace originating in Pelagius, a monk at Bangor-on-Dee. It was opposed by St Augustine of Hippo and the entire Roman Catholic Church, although it was supported by the usurper Vortigern, ruler of Britain after the departure of the Romans around 410. So strictly did the Church oppose the heresy, in fact, that the wave of pagan Picts and Scots and Saxons currently overwhelming Britain was not considered nearly as significant, and St Germanus was dispatched to combat it without the political anarchy of the region entering his remit. Nevertheless, St Germanus' mission is mainly remembered for its "Alleluia Victory" over the pagan hordes, which Welsh tradition relates occurred at Maes Garmon ("The Field of Germanus") near Moel Famau, just across the Dee from Wirral. In the words of the Venerable Bede;

The Saxons and Picts, with their united forces, made war upon the Britons, who in these straits were compelled to take up arms. In their terror thinking themselves unequal to their enemies, they implored the assistance of the holy bishops; who, hastening to them as they had promised, inspired so much confidence into these fearful people, that one would have thought they had been joined by a mighty army. Thus, by these apostolic leaders, Christ Himself commanded in their camp. *The holy days of Lent were also at hand, and were rendered more sacred by the presence of the bishops, insomuch that the people being instructed by daily sermons, came together eagerly to receive the grace of baptism. For a great multitude of the army desired admission to the saving waters, and a wattled church was constructed for the Feast of the Resurrection of our Lord, and so fitted up for the army in the field as if it were in a city. Still wet with the baptismal water the troops set forth; the faith of the people was fired; and where arms had been deemed of no avail, they looked to the help of God. News reached the enemy of the manner and method of their purification, who, assured of success, as if they had to deal with an unarmed host, hastened forward with renewed eagerness. But their approach was made known by scouts. When, after the celebration of Easter, the greater part of the army, fresh from the font, began to take up arms and prepare for war, Germanus offered to be their leader. He picked out the most active, explored the country round about, and observed, in the way by which the enemy was expected, a valley encompassed by hills of moderate height. In that place he drew up his untried troops, himself acting as their general. And now a formidable host of foes drew near, visible, as they approached, to his men lying in ambush. Then, on a sudden, Germanus, bearing the standard, exhorted his men, and bade them all in a loud voice repeat his words. As the enemy advanced in all security, thinking to take them by surprise, the bishops three times cried, "Hallelujah." A universal shout of the same word followed, and the echoes from the surrounding hills gave back the cry on all sides, the enemy was panic-stricken, fearing, not only the neighbouring rocks, but even the very frame of heaven above them; and such was their terror, that their feet were not swift enough to save them. They fled in disorder, casting away their arms, and well satisfied if, even with unprotected bodies, they could escape the danger;*

many of them, flying headlong in their fear, were engulfed by the river which they had crossed. The Britons, without a blow, inactive spectators of the victory they had gained, beheld their vengeance complete. The scattered spoils were gathered up, and the devout soldiers rejoiced in the success which Heaven had granted them. The prelates thus triumphed over the enemy without bloodshed, and gained a victory by faith, without the aid of human force. Thus, having settled the affairs of the island, and restored tranquillity by the defeat of the invisible foes, as well as of enemies in the flesh, they prepared to return home. Their own merits, and the intercession of the blessed martyr Alban, obtained for them a calm passage, and the happy vessel restored them in peace to the desires of their people.

In Welsh tradition, however, the leader of the pagans was Benlli, an Irishman, who is said to have had his castle in the hill fort just south of Moel Famau, known to this day as Foel Fenlli (Benlli's Hill), which was "consumed by fire" at the prayer of St Germanus. The only man to survive was Cadell of the Gleaming Hilt, grandson of the usurper Vortigern yet as righteous a man as Lot. After being blessed by St Germanus, he went on to found a dynasty that ruled Powys.

It is believed that St Hilary's in Wallasey was dedicated by St Germanus himself, or possibly by one of his followers, about 446 AD, some years after the battle. At first, like the church described above, and like the first church at Glastonbury, it was no doubt a "wattled church[4]," but later it was rebuilt—repeatedly—in stone.

***

---

[4] *Built of wattle and daub.*

In 1727, Wallasey schoolmaster Henry Robinson wrote a letter to a Mr Bunbury in which he related all that he had heard about the origins of Wallasey, both the village and its parish church. His sources were Parson Glover, from West Kirby, Richard Watt of Wallasey and Robert Wilson from Liscard.

He said that long ago, the chief man in the area was named Wally, who lived where Stanny's House stood in Robinson's own day. His church, or kirk, stood in the churchyard of St Hilary's, the current parish church, and Wallasey Village was then called Kirby Wally.

Robinson added that the name Wallasey came into being when invaders of Britain reached this western promontory and asked the natives to whom the sea beyond belonged. The natives informed them that it was Wally's Sea, and so the village became known by that name too, although it later became Wallasey. Wally was also lord of Poulton, and so the inlet nearby became known as Wallasey Pool.

Wally's son died without leaving an heir and his daughter married the lord of Litherland. So Wallasey came into the possession of the Litherland family.

Another great man in the area was Lee, who owned a church near Kirkway in Liscard, which was then named Lee's Kirk. Lee owned land on Bidston Moss where he grazed his cattle. If for any reason he could not return home in the evening, he would loose them on the Leasowe, which was then called Wally's Lee's Way. The church fell into disuse while Wallasey's church lacked a priest.

Since Lee's Kirk was no longer in use, it was demolished, and the materials were taken to Wally's Kirk where they were used to construct one great church. It still stood in Henry Robinson's day, although all that remains now of any pre nineteenth century church is the old tower, built in 1530. Near the south door stood the highly ornamented Weeping Cross, so-called because here the priests met the funeral processions. It was vandalised during the English Civil War and further by William of Orange's men during the Glorious Revolution, before being used for the steps of a style.

Wally and Lee were both vassals of the Baron of Halton, and in their day Bidston Moss was a wood. As mentioned at the start, in Robinson's time old people said that a man might have gone from treetop to treetop from Meols to Birkenhead. Even in Robinson's days, tree trunks were found in the peat of Bidston Moss, as well as out under the sea at Meols Stocks (see the chapter on Meols).

During the several stages of the construction of the church at Wallasey, groups of strangers came to work on it, sometimes for a week, sometimes for a fortnight, after which they went away without asking for pay or reward. A master workman and several workers provided and dressed stone to build one of the arches of the church. When they left without asking for any pay, and people asked them where they came from, they answered mysteriously, "Out of the wood."

The Legend of the Boot

The Boot Inn, Liscard, preserves the following legend, which is attached to the very jackboot that gives the inn its name:

Our good Queen Bess did rule this realm, when honest Jack was host unto this inn, well helped by lusty wife and buxom daughter Joan. One wild dark night when all were snoring snug abed, a fierce wild horseman, bedaubed with muck and blood, did gallop to the door, making a thunderous thump thereon; when our host did open unto him, he rushed into the house, a big jack boot in one hand, and a great horse pistol in the other, calling wild foul words for instant meat and drink.

He had a beastly savage look, and our host did eye him well while meat and drink went bolting down his wolfish maw. Thinks Jack, there's booty in that boot, *for when he thumped it on the board there was a chink of gold, the pistol too was by.*

Our honest Jack was 'cute and bold' and when he brought more wine he wilful spilt it on the man, and when he turned in wrath Jack whipped the pistol to his sconce and called for lusty wife and buxom Joan, and they did bind the robber safe and sure, and made the gold lined boot secure.

This scarce well done when in bounced three gentlemen, one with bloody sconce and bootless leg, who when he saw the robber bound was glad, but soon began to wail his boot. Now did our host begin to crow and bid his women bring the gold lined boot. The gentleman was then in hearty mood and gave ten guineas to our host, ten more to lusty wife and buxom Joan. He gave the robber to the gibbet, and the boot to be a sign unto this Inn while it does stand.

-J Bramwell

The Witch's Revenge

The Magazine Hotel in Wallasey is reputed to be cursed by a witch. After a fire in 2010 an article in the local newspaper reported the owners' conviction that the disaster was linked with the theft of a small image of a witch that hung from the ceiling in the main bar. Along with another witch and a devil, all made of brown felt, it had hung there for a hundred years; all three were covered in dust and cobwebs because of the curse that fell on anyone who touched them. After the witch was stolen, the hotel was the scene of a terrible fire, and although the other witch and the devil survived the conflagration, they too went missing shortly afterwards. Two of the pub's regulars replaced the witch with one bought in Pendle.

Tom Slemen, in his book *Haunted Wirral*, tells another story.

The Magazine Hotel was haunted by the ghost of a witch from Liscard, who was tortured and flung into the Mersey with rocks tied to her. Despite this, her body was found washed ashore, and was taken to the Hotel for the inquest. She was found to be still breathing and she recovered sufficiently to offer to reward her rescuers by teaching them her powers, including how to sell their souls to the Devil. Presumably she died shortly after, although the story is vague on this point. Certainly her ghost was said to haunt the hotel—and apparently does to this present day!

The Wreckers

Since time immemorial, the people of coastal regions believed that they were entitled to claim ownership any items washed up on the shore. In fact, all salvage is legally the property of the Crown, although the Receiver of Wreck will pay any salvers who give up the salvage they have found to the authorities. However, this law has seldom been efficiently enforced, and "wrecking" — the plundering of cargoes belonging to wrecked ships — has been reported up to the present day.

But the wrecking for which Wirral was notorious, coming second only to Cornwall in infamy (and continuing for forty years after being stamped out in the southwest), was a form of piracy that involved luring ships with "false lights" onto rocks with the intent of wrecking them to plunder their cargo. According to many sources, this was a major source of wealth for the people of the North Wirral coast, particularly Wallasey Village. A local saying is recorded:

Wallasey for wreckers,
Poulton for trees,
Liscard for honest men,
And Seacombe for thieves.

Other accounts state that the wreckers would interfere with navigational lights to lure ships off course. Hilda Gamlin records that:

The coast was infested with wreckers. Their method of alluring a vessel to destruction was to tie up one leg of a donkey, and place a lantern upon its head, and then urge it along on the hills. The limp caused by the crippled limb caused the lantern to rock to and fro, giving effect in the distance to the sway of a light at a masthead, and thus craft at sea were deceived and wrecked, their cargo becoming the spoil of those who had set the decoy...

Ships are said to have been lured to their doom by fires lit on the beach and hills to confuse the captain's bearings.

On hearing that a ship had been run aground, the wreckers would hurry to the shore with horses, wheelbarrows, and handcarts. They waded into the water carrying axes, and would then bash in the hull until the timbers parted and were carried away by the heavy seas. The wreckers would club survivors on the head, or kick them back into the sea. If a washed-up body had valuables in its pockets they would take them, and if it had a ring on one of its fingers, the wreckers would not hesitate to cut it off the corpse's finger.

During an inquest into deaths by drowning at the time of the Elizabeth Buckham wreck in 1866, the coroner quoted a prayer supposedly taught to young children in earlier days:

God bless feyther and God bless mather,
And God send us a wreck afore morning.

He also repeated a tale that relates how one Sunday, when a wreck was reported in St. Hilary's Church in Wallasey Village, the rector himself said: 'Keep your seats till after the collection and then we can all start fair,' before leading the wreckers across the sandhills.

Mother Redcap

In the eighteenth and early nineteenth century all of North Wirral was remote and cut off from more densely inhabited areas. Wallasey was more isolated than most, and it gained a notorious reputation as a haunt of smugglers and pirates.

The headquarters of local smuggling was a house that once stood on what is now Egremont Promenade, between Lincoln Drive and Caithness Drive. Built in 1595 by one of the Mainwaring family, on the shore just above the high-water mark, beside what was at that time bleak, desolate Liscard Moor, it went through a number of different names including the Half-Way House, the Whitehouse and Seabank Nook. Next to it were three houses called Seabank Cottages. It became a port-of-call for privateers and fishermen, and a place where Liverpool pilots could board vessels.

The house became a tavern during the American War of Independence, when American and English privateers roamed the high seas. The tavern was nicknamed Mother Redcap's after its owner, an elderly lady called Poll Jones who always wore a red cap or bonnet. Mother Redcap was a great friend to smugglers and privateers, gaining a reputation as the "foster mother of wild spirits." The tavern was rebuilt as both a hiding place for smuggled goods, and a potential death-trap for unwary customs men.

Mother Redcap had been a handsome woman in former years, and was believed to be a widow. She had a pretty niece who helped her in her work and was much admired by the young mariners who drank in the tavern, despite her offhand manner, although she later married a revenue man. Mother Redcap herself was very likeable, and assisted sailors by acting as a banker, minding their earnings while they were at sea. Many of the clientele came from the crews of privateers who anchored at Red Bets, the anchorage opposite the tavern, and rowed over to drink and exchange stories.

Crewmen hid from the Royal Navy pressgangs in the

inn until their ships were ready to sail. The rooms upstairs were divided by screens rather than walls, and there was no ceiling, just the underside of the roof. The smugglers hid contraband in the walls and ceilings of lower rooms. In one wall there was a secret hiding place for a man, with an entrance from the floor of the above room.

When the coast was clear, they moved contraband secretly, probably at night, over Liscard Moor behind the inn and through or round Liscard, along Wallasey Road and down Breck Road, then down the old footpath to Bidston and out on to Bidston Moss where the road ended. This was a hazardous route, but the only way round was via Green Lane, Wallasey, and past Leasowe Castle.

Mother Redcap's was built of red free-stone, and the walls were practically three feet thick. There were two mullioned windows at the front, and the walls were covered by thick planks of wood from wrecked ships. Eventually this timbering fell off, at some point before 1857, when the first painting of the tavern was made; it was never replaced. There was a front door made of five inch thick oak, studded with iron nails, and seems to have had several sliding bars across the inside. Just inside the door was a trapdoor leading down to the cellar under the north room, a rough wooden lid with hinges and shackles. An intruder forcing the front door would automatically withdraw the bolt of the trapdoor, precipitating the unwelcome visitor into the cellar, eight or nine feet below. It was also used for depositing goods.

If a visitor had successfully negotiated this initial obstacle, they would have the options of entering a room to the north or another to the south (although this entrance would be covered by the open front door), or going straight up a staircase directly ahead of the door. The main entrance into the cellar was behind this staircase, where seven or eight steps led down. At the top of the cellar steps, a narrow doorway led out into the yard at the back. Behind the stairs was also a door leading into a kitchen at the back of the house, from which the yard was also accessible.

The beams in the two main rooms of the house were made of oak, and the chimney breasts were very large inside. There were cavities near the ceiling, over the oak beams that had removable entrances from the top of the chimney breasts inside the flues. In the wall were other smaller cavities where Mother Redcap kept the earnings of sailors and also the prize money of privateer crews while they were at sea.

In the yard was a well, twelve foot deep, dry and partly filled in with earth. On the west side of the wall of the well (facing inland) there was a hole that seemed to lead into the garden but probably led to a mysterious passage. Also at the back of the house was a small stream, supplying the house and also used by the boats that anchored nearby. A brew-house was also to be found in the yard, and the place was noted for its homebrewed ale as late as 1840.

At the south end of the house there was another cave or cellar, and a mosaic was placed over sandstone flags that covered this cavity. A square hole with steps, made to look like a dry pit well, was the entrance to this cellar. Much of the yard seems to have been hollow, flagstones on beams covering a large subterranean space. A manure heap and a stock of coal were piled on top of it; the coal was brought in small boats called "flats" and Mother Redcap sold it to the people of Liscard. When contraband was concealed inside the cave, the coal and barrels were moved to cover the entrance.

Beneath the yard was a large cave, used for concealing contraband, and at its end was the entrance to the tunnel mentioned previously. Rumours claim that this passage joined up with others, leading to locations as far away as the Yellow Noses in New Brighton, and the priory in Birkenhead.

More conservative accounts say that it led to an opening in a ditch that led to a pit about halfway up what is now Lincoln Drive, in the direction of Liscard. On the edge of this pit grew a willow tree which was used as a lookout post from which one of Mother Redcap's confederates could survey the whole entrance to the Mersey.

The shore in front of the house was made up of pebbles and star grass, and had stone sidewalls running down to the strand on either side, to counter the flood-tide. The north wall, which was very strong, was used as a shelter for boats and had thick wooden posts on its top where boards could be slid to increase the wall's height. Despite these precautions it was not unknown for the cellar to be flooded at high tide when there was a north west gale.

On the shore in front of the house was a wooden seat made from timbers taken from wrecked ships. On one end of this was a short flagpole topped by what appeared to be a wind vane. In reality it was used by the smugglers to signal danger when the vane pointed away from the house. On the other end of the seat another post held a picture of Mother Redcap holding a frying pan over a fire, and underneath were the words:

> *All ye that are weary come in an' take rest,*
> *Our eggs and our ham they are of the best,*

Our ale and our porter are likewise the same,
Step in if you please and give 'em a name.
                              -Mother Redcap.

An old song about Mother Redcap went:

Who's Mother Redcap? Mistress Poll.
She wore a bedcap on her knoll.
She lived in an inn of wood and stones,
Old Mother Redcap, Mother Jones.

All the sailors came to her inn
to eat her bread and drink her gin.
Old Mother Redcap gave them a bed;
She gave them shelter and kept them fed.

There the men were safe and sound;
when dread and pressgangs were around,
Old Mother Redcap bolted her door
and hid them underneath the floor.

Stories of Smuggling

1. Right Of Way

Some time back in the eighteenth century there was a great dispute at Mother Redcap's concerning right-of-way. A dead body had been found on the beach and it was carried into the tavern by the back door. For superstitious reasons, when it was removed again for burial, it was taken out by the front door. The customs men claimed that the passing of the body through the house made it a right-of-way, and that people could go through at any time of the day or night. When they attempted to put this into practice, a fierce fight resulted.

2. A Rum Business

Another time a local customs officer got wind of a consignment of contraband rum that the smugglers were bringing in through Mother Redcap's. His informant told him that the smugglers intended to take two barrels round the Moss by donkey cart to the Ring O' Bells in Bidston (from which it would be distributed to interested parties throughout Wirral).

The customs officer concealed himself along the track the carter would take, and leapt out on the man when he appeared.

"You've got rum in those kegs!" he cried.

"Nay," the carter replied. "It's ale—they've run out at the Ring O' Bells and I'm taking them some."

The customs man demanded proof and the carter let him inspect the kegs, which did indeed contain ale. Mother Redcap had learnt of the customs man's plans and exchanged the rum for ale.

3. A Body on the Beach

One day, a customs man came to Mother Redcap's and sat in the barroom, talking jovially with the clientele. The smugglers had contraband rum in the cellar, which they were anxious to move on, but the man's presence made this impossible. As the evening drew on they awaited his departure with growing impatience, but still he showed no sign of leaving.

One of the smugglers had a plan. He left the tavern by the back way and went down to the sand. Here he lay, pretending to be a drowned man. Meanwhile, another smuggler who was in on the plan entered the barroom and reported a body on the beach. The customs officer, filled with professional zeal, went down to investigate. The moment he was gone, the smugglers took the rum up from the cellar and swiftly took it off.

The customs man investigated the corpse, and found the man's watch and chain. When he tried to take it, the "corpse" rose up and hit him. A commotion broke out and the customs man demanded to know what was going on. The smuggler told him he had been walking along the shore when a sudden fit had seized him, and he had known no more until he found himself—as he thought—being robbed.

Meanwhile, the contraband rum was halfway to Bidston.

The Smugglers' Way

When the smugglers at Mother Redcap's were sure that the coast was clear, they would transport their contraband across Liscard Moor (between the Egremont shore and Liscard Village), through or round Liscard, and then down onto Bidston Moss. In those days, before the Moss was drained, this was a perilous route, and one safe path alone led across the otherwise trackless wilderness. Naturally enough, only the smugglers knew it.

It led across a partially submerged bridge known as the Jaw Bones, because it was made from the jawbones of a whale. The whole Moss was said to be haunted, but that spot in particular was known for the ghosts of two smugglers, who died there in the pursuit of their unlawful occasions. It is said that the waters of the Moss still contain lost riches.

Should the smugglers successfully cross the Jaw Bones, they would follow a rough track towards Bidston Village, bringing them to a tavern called the Ring O' Bells (now Stone Farm), where they sold it to the landlord, who concealed it in his outbuildings. From here the landlord would distribute it through the rest of Wirral via a packhorse track to Noctorum, then along a narrow road and finally along Roman Road in Prenton.

The Ring O' Bells itself earned a notoriety almost as great as Mother Redcap's; under its later landlord Simon Croft, who is reputed to have inspired the song "Simon the Cellarer," it became a popular haunt for ne'er-do-wells and prize fighters, until the local landowner revoked the license in 1868. See the chapter on Bidston for more details.

Mother Redcap's Treasure

Mother Redcap was something of a public benefactor, and provided many other services than her thick, brown ale and assistance to smugglers. Her tavern was also a place of refuge for sailors on the run from the pressgang and as previously stated, she provided banking facilities for the crews of the privateer ships that used to moor nearby. It is said that she had vast sums of money concealed, and shortly before her death a privateer had come into port with a prize so rich that each crewman had earned at least a thousand pounds. Mother Redcap received a great deal of this for safekeeping. She died shortly after, and despite a rigorous search, not a penny of the prize money was found. Its location remains a mystery to this day.

The only possible clue as to its eventual fate was found in the mid-nineteenth century, when a quantity of guineas were discovered in a cavity near the shore, at the location known ever since as "Guinea Gap." But this haul cannot represent the whole of Mother Redcap's treasure.

The Captain's Pit

A recently-married sea captain took his bride to live at the long-vanished Liscard Castle, a nineteenth century folly. The captain returned to sea and his wife remained at the house, awaiting his return. One day, however, the news came to her that her husband had gone down with his ship and was drowned.

She was so shocked by this news that she ran from the house and flung herself into the flooded pit in Hose Side Road, hoping that by drowning she would join her lost husband. This is how the Captain's Pit got its name.

After her tragic death, the lady's spirit walked in the old house. A master workman was employed to supervise the blocking up of several smugglers' tunnels that had been found in the cellar. These tunnels were said to run as far as the Red Noses, New Brighton, in one direction, and St. Hilary's Church in Wallasey Village in the other.

One day, after his workers had left, the master workman heard a knocking from the cellar. Afraid that someone had been accidentally walled up, he rushed down to the cellar and shouted, "Who's there?" but there was no reply except the continued knocking.

Overcome by fear, he ran up the steps and returned to the daylight, shaking with fear.

Leasowe Castle

Leasowe Castle, originally known as Newhall, was built in 1593 by Ferdinando, the fifth Earl of Derby, a patron of Shakespeare and a descendant of Sir John Stanley (see the chapter on Storeton) who some believe wrote the medieval poem *Sir Gawayne and the Grene Knight*. He had the octagonal tower built to watch the Wallasey races (forerunners of the more famous Derby). Ferdinando died young, according to some people the victim of witchcraft, and the building became the property of the Egerton family, who only occasionally occupied it; Ferdinando's brother and successor, William, the sixth Earl of Derby (who some maintain wrote the works of William Shakespeare), settled in Bidston, where he built Bidston Hall. According to local legend, during the Civil War Leasowe Castle fell into Parliamentary hands, and it was subsequently besieged by the Royalists. Eventually it fell into disrepair, becoming known to sailors as Mockbeggar[5] Hall

The Wallasey races are said to have been "probably the oldest gentleman's racecourse in the kingdom." Stories say that James I attended the races, and there is no doubt that the Duke of Monmouth won a race at Leasowe while touring the western counties courting popularity prior to the ill-fated Monmouth Rising. The story goes that after winning the race, (which is widely believed to have been fixed in his favour), he offered the opposing jockey a chance at revenge in the form of a

[5] *A not uncommon name in coastal regions, possibly Celtic in origin, although it is also a name mentioned in a nineteenth century list of folklore ghosts and monsters. Leasowe Castle is famous for its ghost (see The Ghost Room).*

foot-race, which he also won.

However, this was all contrived to draw attention away from the secret meetings between his advisers and the heads of their supporters who had gathered at Bidston Hall, and included the squires of Thurstaston and Gayton, among others. Only the previous month the conspirators implicated in the Ryehouse Plot had been executed, and Monmouth was on the run. He was arrested on his return to Court, and released on bail.

The Ghost Room

Returning to Leasowe Castle, there is a room on the mezzanine level between first and second floors called the Boardroom, also known as the Oak Room, or the Ghost Room. Octagonal in shape, it is lit by two windows set in the thick walls and it is panelled from floor to ceiling, although originally the walls were rough-hewn stone.

At some point in the building's history, the owners became embroiled in a family feud with another noble line. They took prisoner the head of the rival family and his young son, who they shut up in the Oak Room. Fearing that their captors would torture them, the father smothered his son then killed himself by dashing out his brains against the wall.

The building has been a hotel several times during its chequered history, and the room itself was at one point a bedroom. A visitor, who had heard nothing of the story related above, made "a terrible hullabaloo at midnight," saying that he had seen a man and a boy standing in the moonlight between his bed and the windows.

"Sea Come Not Hither…"

In the days of Ethelred the Unready, England was in trouble. The Danes and their king Swein Forkbeard came time and time again, looting and burning, and each time the king bought them off with money raised by the tax known as the Danegeld. When King Ethelred saw that this only encouraged the Danes to come again and again, he plotted against the Danes already in the kingdom and had them all murdered on St. Brice's Day, 13th November, 1002. One of the victims of this massacre was the sister of King Swein, and when the news reached his ears, the Danish king led an army to England to avenge her.

During the ensuing war, King Ethelred fled his country and sought refuge in Normandy, leaving Swein king of all England. But Swein died the next year and the war continued between his son Canute and Ethelred's son Edmund Ironside. In the end, they divided the kingdom between them, with Canute ruling the North and Edmund the South. Edmund soon died and Canute became king of all England as well as Denmark. Ten years later, he extended his empire to include Norway.

Canute had many courtiers who flattered him on the strength of this wide empire, and claimed that he ruled both the land and the waves. This angered the king, and he decided to teach them a lesson. One day while in the north of his kingdom, he came to Leasowe, where the sea often flooded the land. He told his servants to place his throne down on the beach, where he sat surrounded by his flatterers, though they kept a worried eye on the waves.

The tide turned, and came flooding in, and the

courtiers suggested he move his throne further up the beach. Canute said, "I do not wish to move. You tell me that I rule the waves as well as the land; very well. I shall command them. Sea, come not hither," he cried, addressing the waters, "nor wet the sole of my foot!"

Yet the rebellious sea paid him no heed: the waves came in and the courtiers' fine clothes were drenched. Together with the king, they made an undignified retreat inland. Standing on the sandhills, looking back across the sea, Canute said, "God alone is master of the sea."

The courtiers were so ashamed of their foolish talk that they never flattered him again.

Until the mid-twentieth century, a chair sat at Leasowe Castle, with the words that Canute had uttered carved upon its back. It was finally broken up and used as firewood. The tide that regularly used to flood Leasowe is now held back by concrete sea defences.

The Leasowe Mermaid

An entire cycle of stories relates to a mermaid who was sighted off Leasowe, or Wallasey, in the eighteenth and nineteenth century. The first account was written down in an eighteenth century chapbook. Entitled 'The Wonder of Wonders,' the story describes the adventures of one John Robinson, mariner, who encountered a mermaid on the Black Rock 'nigh Liverpool,' and it goes as follows:

On the 29th April last one Mr James Dixon captain and commander of the ship Dolin in her passage from Amsterdam in Holland, was beat back by a tempestuous wind and all the men perished except a young man named John Robinson, who was taken very ill on board the ship, and was left by almighty providence, and to the mercy of the seas and winds, and was also in great fear and dreadful fright on the main ocean, for the said John Robinson dreamt that he was on the top of an high mountain, whose top he thought reached up to the heavens, and that there was a fine castle, about the circumference of a mile, and furnished with all sorts of diamonds, and precious stones, and likewise on the top of the mountain was a well, which water was as sweet as honey and as white as milk, that whomsoever drank of that water should never be dry again; with all sorts of music very delightful to hear, so one would think, as one supposed seven years in that place, not so long as a day.

After having viewed the castle round he observed to his great admiration, a beautiful young lady, who was guarded by seven serpents, very frightful to behold.

Supposing the young lady was very beautiful, yet he wished rather to be a thousand miles off than in the sight of those serpents; and looking round about, he espied (to his great comfort) a green gate, and a street paved with blue marble, which opened at his coming to it, and so he got away from the serpents; but coming to the top of the hill, he did not know how to get down, it being very high and steep, but he found a ladder to his comfort; it being very slender, was afraid to venture, but at last was obliged to go down it, for one of the serpents having taken notice of him pursued him so very close that he was in great danger, and thought he fell and broke his leg, and that the serpent fell upon him, which awaked him in great fright, and almost made him mad.

By this you may think what a great trouble he was in, awaked alone on the main ocean, when missing all the rest of the ship's crew, and also the great danger he was in.

But to his great amazement, he espied a beautiful young lady combing her head, and tossed on the billows, clothed all in green (but by chance he got the first word with her) then she with a smile came on board and asked how he did. The young man being something smart and a scholar, replied, "Madam, I am the better to see you in good health, in great hopes trusting you will be a comfort and assistance to me in this my low condition"; and so caught hold of her comb and green girdle that was about her waist. To which she replied, "Sir, you ought not to rob a young woman of her riches, and then expect a favour at her hands; but if you will give me my comb and girdle again, what lies in my power, I will do for you."

At which time he had no power to keep them from her, but immediately delivered them up again; she then smiling, thanked him, and told him, if he would meet her again next Friday she would set him on shore. He had no power to deny her, so readily gave his consent; at which time she gave him a compass and desired him to steer south west; he thanked her and told her he wanted some news. She said she would tell him the next opportunity when he fulfilled his promises; but that he would find his father and mother much grieved about him, and so jumping into the sea she departed out of his sight.

At her departure the tempest ceased and blew a fair gale to south west, so he got safe on shore; but when he came to his father's house he found everything as she had told him. for she told him also concerning his being left on ship board, and how all the seamen perished, which he found all true what she had told him, according to the promise made him.

He was still very much troubled in his mind,

concerning his promise, but yet while he was thus musing, she appeared to him with a smiling countenance and (by his misfortune) she got the first word of him, so that he could not speak one word, but was quite dumb, yet he took notice of the words she spoke; and she began to sing. After which she departed out of the young man's sight, taking from him the compass.

She took a ring from off her finger, and put it on the young man's, and said, she expected to see him once again with more freedom. but he never saw her more, upon which he came to himself again, went home, and was taken ill, and died in five days after, to the wonderful admiration of all people who saw the young man.

***

It is unclear what is meant by 'the Black Rock.' This was the old name for what is now called Perch Rock, now home to the famous fort which guards the entrance to the Mersey. Older accounts, however, including the 1610 map of Wirral by the cartographer Speed, refer to a 'Black Rock' on the shore of Leasowe, and as we will see, later accounts of mermaids in these waters link her with this area.

Tom Slemen records an account from 1848 of another young mariner, Richard Mattaign, who was supposedly rescued from the wreck of the *Ocean Monarch*, off Great Orme in North Wales, by a naked woman "with a very pale complexion and long black hair" who left him on the shore at Hoylake before walking back into the sea. Mattaign was sure that the woman had been a mermaid, but no one believed him other than an old sailor named

O'Connell, who had often seen merfolk off the Leasowe coast.

Mattaign found work in Leasowe, and here he reencountered the mermaid while swimming off the shore. She was guarded by a seal and a swordfish with a blue diamond mark between its eyes. One day, three men came from the sea and took the mermaid with them, and Mattaign never saw her again.

Mattaign ended up in the Mariners' Home in Wallasey, and despite his requests for a burial at sea, after his death his body was consigned to a pauper's grave. A month after his death, a swordfish was caught off Perch Rock. Between its eyes was a strange blue diamond-shaped mark...

Finally, at the shore by Leasowe Castle there was once a board that recorded another legend. The story said that on when the tide was full and the moon shone in the sky, at midnight a mermaid could be seen on the nearby boulders known as 'The Mermaid's Stones.'

Games and Traditions

After harvest time came the cake play. In those days, after reaping, people went gleaning—picking up the grain that had been left behind by the reapers. This grain was milled and the resulting flour was baked into cakes by the wife of "some respectable labouring man." The cake play went on at a private house, never the local alehouse. The details of the game are not known, but the participants each paid a nominal fee and the winner received the cakes.

More is known about the prison bar play. This took place in open air and during the day, usually at open land that existed then at Leasowe, or on Liscard Moor, or Meols. Teams came from each township and played against each other as local cricket clubs or football clubs do today, for a prize, usually half a barrel of ale which was shared by both the winning side and the losers. During the game, one team stood in a ring, surrounded by the other team. They would go round in circles, and one by one, members of each team would pursue someone from the other, with the intention of "ticking" them. The same game, or one very similar, is mentioned by the *Encyclopaedia Britannica* as named variously "prisoner's base, also called base, bars, or prison bars" in which "players of one team seek to tag and imprison players of the other team who venture out of their home territory, or base." It goes on to say that it is mentioned in 14th century French writing and that it was probably one of the most popular games in the Middle Ages. It is also referred to in the supposed diary of Elizabeth Woodville, Edward IV's queen, (actually a forgery of the nineteenth century). Games of "tick" and the notion of "bases" in games were still current in Wirral of the early 1980s. Another idea common to these games was that of being "barley" if one was on a "base"; you could not be ticked while "barley.". The author remembers, as a child, being told by grownups that this word was a corruption of the medieval word "parley."

Other amusements available include the horse races in the Big Croft, a field in Upton. Oxton also hosted races, but these were foot races or donkey races. Caldy had a Maypole. "Shows" were also popular, and these seem to have included clowns, since one is known to have featured a "Mountebag," or mountebank. Indoors, there was "sewing," although precisely what this was is unknown. Raffles were also popular. Outdoors there was cock-fighting, and a cockpit[6] is still to be seen on Bidston Hill, and bull-baiting. "Murryneet" or Merry Night, was popular; this was a meeting where each of the guests contributed a sum for the benefit of the person putting on the entertainment.

Another popular game at harvest time was neck-cutting, which despite the gruesome name was something very similar to Harvest Home or Winning the Churn in other areas. The last few stalks of grain in a field were plaited into a band of three stands, and the reapers threw their sickles at it; the winner was the one who finally cut it down. Not surprisingly, there were frequent accidents, and as a result it became less popular.

As in many places, Shrove Tuesday was kept as a carnival, a farewell to meat. On the following day (Ash Wednesday), the fasting populace ate "furmenty", or frumenty, shelled wheat boiled in new milk with sugar and spice. It was popular at all Wirral festivities. Easter itself was celebrated with eggs, and a popular custom was pace-egging, examples of which will be mentioned in the chapters on Thurstaston and Neston.

---

[6] *Formerly a gorse mill.*

13
BIDSTON

And so we come to Bidston, a goodly house, desmesne, and park of the right honourable William Earl of Derby; which, though it be less than many other seats which his honour hath, wherein to make his residences when he is so pleased; yet for the pleasant situation of this, and the variety of noble delights appendent to it, his lordship seems much to affect the same, and enlargeth the conveniences therein for his pleasure and abode many ways, which, with craving pardon for my bold collections, I suppose his honour doth out of his honourable love to this our county, that we might have the more of his presence here, where he bears the great places of his Majesty's lord lieutenant, in the causes military, and the Prince's highness, chamberlain of the county palatine,- as his noble and worthy ancestors have done before him.

Bidston Hall

As mentioned above, Bidston Hall was built by William, the sixth Earl of Derby, after he succeeded his brother Ferdinando, the builder of Leasowe Castle. William was abroad when his brother died, during an adventurous time in his life that was chronicled in a ballad entitled *Sir William Stanley's Travels* (see Appendix 2), which claims that he travelled far and wide, (other sources say he was accompanied by the poet John Donne); to France, Spain, Italy, Germany, Egypt, Morocco, Barbary, Russia, the Holy Land, Turkey, Greenland, Holland, and back to Merry England.

It had been quite a gap year (in fact, it was three years); in Egypt he fought and killed a tiger, in Turkey he narrowly escaped death for insulting Mohammed, (being released because a local Muslim lady had fallen in love with him); and on returning home from Greenland in a whaling ship he had to fight a lengthy lawsuit against his eldest niece, who claimed her father's estates, including Lathom, Knowsley, and the Isle of Man.

Once William had settled this matter, exhausted by all his adventures, he delegated the running of his estates to his son, James, Lord Strange, (later to become the so-called Great Earl of Derby, staunch supporter of the King during the English Civil War) and retired to Bidston, which, as his contemporary William Webb says above, was his favourite residence. He passed his summers in Bidston and his winters at Stanley Palace in Chester, devoting much of his time to playwriting. None of his writings survive, although he is said by some to have been the true author of Shakespeare's works. In Bidston, Shakespeare is referred to darkly as 'the plagiarist.'

It was also where William's grandson Charles, eighth Earl of Derby, "lived quietly" after his late father's involvement in the English Civil War. This had resulted in much of the Derby estates in ruins, sold, or sequestered. Charles remained here until 1659 when he joined Booth's rising, an attempt by the Royalists led by Sir George Booth to overthrow the Commonwealth in the uncertainty following Cromwell's death. The rebellion was crushed at the battle of Winnington Bridge, near Northwich, and Charles was accused of high treason by Parliament. However, he was restored as earl the following year when the monarchy itself was restored, and some of the family's lands were returned to him.

Sometime after these momentous events, Bidston Hall was sold, and at a later date it was won and lost at cards, by the ace of clubs. In memory of this event, a summerhouse was built in the shape of a club, and in the nineteenth century, the building's foundations remained in the hall's grounds, and was rebuilt as Club House, the redbrick building on Bidston Hill that can be seen for miles around. The gambling is also said to have been referred to in the images of three upturned wine glasses on top of the gates. Eventually, the hall came into the possession of the Vyner family, goldsmiths from London.

Bidston Hall is reputed to be Wirral's most haunted building, with tenuous links to Jack the Ripper and Alex Sanders, "king of the witches", who was born in Moon Street in Birkenhead (a street that seems to have been spirited away; until 1940 it lay between Exmouth Street and Bentinck Street but was destroyed during the Blitz). Female visitors to the bedrooms of the hall have reported "unwelcome attention" from ghosts, and the cellars are also said to be haunted. It featured on the television programme *Most Haunted Live* under the alias Bidston Lodge.

Simon the Cellarer

The Ring O'Bells (now Stone Farm) in Bidston was owned by a local family, known in some sources as the Radleys or in others as the Pendletons. Later on in the mid-nineteenth century, a Miss Radley (or a Mary Pendleton) married a man named Simon Croft, under whose proprietorship the place became almost as infamous as Mother Redcap's, although it retained its established reputation for their ham and eggs, which attracted visitors from all over Wirral at holiday time. The Ring O' Bells had its own motto, which ran thus:

Walk in, my friends and taste my beer and liquor
If your pockets be well stored, you'll find it comes the
quicker;
But for want of that has caused both grief and sorrow,
Therefore you must pay to-day: I will trust to-morrow.

Simon Croft

It is described in Albert Smith's 1847 novel *The Struggles and Adventures of Christopher Tadpole* (See Appendix 3).

Simon Croft, who kept his own pigs to provide the ham, succumbed to the temptation of all landlords and became a noted drunk, while the pub itself attracted a lively and mixed crowd, including prize fighters such as Tom Sayers, Jem Mace and the "Tipton Slasher" who called in on their way to train on Hilbre. No doubt they—and the many drunks for whom the place became notorious—appreciated the contraband wine that Simon sold. He died, no doubt happily, in 1864, and is said to have inspired the song "Simon the Cellarer" (below).

Four years after his death, Lady Cust, daughter of Mrs Boode (see Chapter Six), prevailed upon Mr. Vyner, the lord of the manor, to revoke the Ring O' Bells' license due to the continuing scandal of drunkenness on the Sabbath.

Bidston Village has been "dry" ever since.

Old Simon the cellarer keeps a rare store,
Of Malmsey and Malvoisie
And Cyprus, and who can say how many more!
For a chary old soul is he,
A chary old soul is he.

Of Sack and Canary he never doth fail,
And all the year round there is brewing of ale,
Yet he never aileth, he quaintly doth say,
While he keeps to his sober six flagons a day.
But ho! ho! ho! his nose doth shew
How oft the black Jack to his lips doth go.
But ho! ho! ho! his nose doth shew
How oft the black Jack to his lips doth go.

Dame Margery sits in her own still-room,
And a matron sage is she,
From thence oft at Curfew is wafted a fume;
She says it is Rosemary,
She says it is Rosemary.
But there's a small cupboard behind the back stair,
And the maids say they often see Margery there -
Now Margery says that she grows very old,
And must take a something to keep out the cold!

But ho! ho! ho! old Simon doth know,
Where many a flask of his best doth go.

But ho! ho! ho! old Simon doth know,
Where many a flask of his best doth go.
Old Simon reclines in his high-back'd chair,
And talks about taking a wife;
And Margery often is heard to declare
That she ought to be settled in life,
She ought to be settled in life.

But Margery has (so the maids say) a tongue,
And she's not very handsome, and not very young:
So somehow it ends with a shake of the head,
And Simon he brews him a tankard instead.
While ho! ho! ho! he will chuckle and crow,
What! Marry old Margery? no, no, no!
While ho! ho! ho! He will chuckle and crow,
What! Marry old Margery? no, no, no!

Bidston Hill

Bidston Hill is a nexus for legends, supposedly visited by UFOs, riddled with smugglers' tunnels, and haunted by ghosts, witches, Satanists, and the Devil himself. According to more than one story is the final resting place of the Holy Grail.

Up on the hill near the Observatory, are several rock carvings, including one of a horse, which has a sun symbol on its neck; one of a sun goddess; and another (very worn) of a moon god (or goddess). These are often said to be the work of the Vikings, around 1000 AD. There is no real evidence for this, although Norse mythology certainly includes a sun goddess, Sol, a moon god, Mani, and Arvakr, a horse with solar connections.

Other writers say that the carvings are Gallo-Roman, and alternative traditions suggest they are of Phoenician origin—perhaps produced by Joseph of Arimathea's sailors when he concealed the Holy Grail within the hill, which is said to be the real Wearyall (Wirral) Hill. That's assuming it wasn't Sir Gawain who left the Grail there while passing through on his way to his showdown with the Green Knight. Although authorities such as *Le Morte Darthur* assure us that Sir Gawain was a worldly knight and thus never achieved the Quest of the Sangreal, Wirral tradition maintains that not only did he have the Grail about his person, during his visit to the peninsula he had nothing better to do with it than conceal it within Bidston Hill.

The ruined funerary chapel in Flaybrick Cemetery, on the side of the hill, is also the centre of a cycle of legends. Built as a Nonconformist and Anglican chapel (a Roman Catholic chapel elsewhere in the cemetery has been demolished), its walls contain what appear to be occult or Masonic symbols, including an eye in a pyramid and a six pointed star. Last used for its official purpose in 1975, it is a roofless ruin inhabited by bats and frequented by Satanists.

According to a story current in the North End of Birkenhead, its ruinous nature is linked with the murderer Lock Ah Tam. Lock Ah Tam was a Chinese man who settled in Liverpool in the early twentieth century, where he worked as a superintendent of Chinese sailors. After receiving a blow to the head when attacked by Russians, his personality deteriorated and he became violent and drunken, finally murdering his wife and children by shooting them. The jury rejected a plea of diminished responsibility due to insanity, and he was hanged at Walton Gaol.

His victims were buried in Flaybrick Cemetery, supposedly at the same time as the execution. A deafening thunderclap was heard, or in some versions there was a gust of wind from out of nowhere, at the time of the funeral. Lock Ah Tam haunted the minister who conducted the funeral ceremony, and the man later committed suicide by hanging himself in the now ruined chapel, which burnt down, shortly afterwards. According to other stories, Lock Ah Tam's ghost stalks the path near his victims' grave.

Near Flaybrick Cemetery are the Nanny Goat Mountains, a grandiose name for a sandstone outcrop. Supposedly the name harks back to the Middle Ages when goats were kept there, beyond the pale of the deer park. A fever hospital was built nearby, Birkenhead Infectious Diseases Hospital, and it was haunted by the ghost of a nurse, who could be seen in one of the windows. Tunnels were said to lead from the cellar to Flaybrick Cemetery, supposedly so that corpses of the infected could be taken to the cemetery without risk of spreading infection, and also to the nearby St. James' Church, the 'Holy Doughnut' or 'Church in the roundabout.'

After the old fever hospital was demolished, the Oakwood Estate (known as 'The Nannies' in reference to the Nanny Goat Mountains) was built on the site. The streets of the estate are haunted by the Whistler, a ghost who wanders the night streets whistling. Should you hear him whistling, you know he's coming for you—so run!

In 2003 several reports were made a huge, tawny-furred cat seen in the vicinity of Bidston Hill. Merseyside Police are said to have employed a wildlife liaison officer to investigate the sightings of the Bidston Big Cat, but without result.

In the sixties, several people reported encounters

with wolves on Bidston Hill, often accompanied by a man in medieval clothes. One woman was out walking her dog when the wolf attacked it. The man appeared and shouted at the wolf, which came over to him at once. The medieval man and the wolf vanished as they headed towards Bidston windmill.

Dave Shirley, formerly of the Wirral Psychic and Paranormal Workshop, tells a story of a werewolf on Bidston Hill. The werewolf was the son of the first miller, and his birth was witnessed by a wolf, which damned him to a life of lycanthropy. Due to his preying upon local flocks in his wolf-form, the lord of the manor (William Stanley, mentioned in the section on Bidston Hall) banished him to Hilbre.

Another story recounted by Dave Shirley says that Bidston Hill is inhabited by 'pongies', also referred to as 'hobbits'; little people with an affinity for trees who can be detected by a sudden strong smell of moss. Those who have seen them says they are about three feet high and have green fur 'like astroturf.'

The *Oxford Dictionary of English Folklore* describes similar beings common to Wirral and the Cheshire/Lancashire border, called Poldies. Jacqueline Simpson, noted folklorist and co-author of the dictionary heard a story from a friend who had often visited Wirral during her childhood in the fifties.

Children going to the woods were told to come home before dark, because that was when the Poldies came out. The creatures were guardians of the woods, who punished anyone who damaged the trees by making them have some form of accident. A cousin of the informant deliberately twisted small branches off a tree and threw them away, despite her protests. Shortly afterwards he sprained his ankle, and this was attributed to the Poldies.

Years later, she heard that a building contractor had planned to cut down a wood before beginning developments in the area, but he abandoned his plans due to delays caused by flooding, machines breaking down and other problems. In the opinion of the locals, it was the Poldies defending their homes.

14
MEOLS AND HOYLAKE

Following the circuit of the shire, we come next to Great Meoles, which gives name and seat to an ancient family of Meolses...

The Meols Stocks

The ancient manor of Meols is said to have stood on Dove Point, which has since been washed away by the sea. "Dove" probably comes from the Celtic word "dubh" which means black, referring to the peat bogs that were once seen between Meols and Leasowe. At low water, the remains of a drowned forest were visible. Known locally as the Meolse Stocks, or the Turf Brews, it was first mentioned in 1615, when the following was written:

In these mosses, especially in the black, are fir-trees found under the ground, in some places six feet deep or more, and in others not one foot; which trees are of a surprising length. and straight, having certain small branches like boughs, and roots at one end—as if they had been blown down by winds; and yet no man can tell that ever any such trees did grow there, nor yet how they should come thither. Some are of the opinion that they have lain there ever since Noah's flood.

A poem entitled "Ye Stockes in Worolde" (The Stocks in Wirral), describes them in detail:

But greater wonder calls me hence: ye deepe
Low spongie mosses yet rembrance keepe
Of Noah's flood: on numbers infinite
Of fir trees—swains do in their cesses light;
And in summe places, when the sea doth bate
Down from ye shoare, 'tis wonder to relate
How many thousands of theis trees now stand
Black broken on their rootes, which once drie land
Did cover, whence turfs Neptune yields to showe
He did not always to theis borders flow.

The Sunken Land

Occupation began at a site now under the sea off Meols during the Neolithic period or New Stone Age, but increased exponentially during the Iron Age and the Roman periods. The exact location of the site is a mystery, since it sank gradually beneath the waves over a period stretching from the Neolithic to the nineteenth century. Over the millennia, the North Wirral coast has been receding, and each period in Meols' long history has ended with flood and erosion.

Artefacts collected along the shore suggest the

existence from 500 BC onwards of a significant port with far-flung trade links. Coins have been found that originated among the Coriosolites, an Iron Age tribe of Brittany, while others come from as far away as pre-Roman Carthage, Augustan Rome, and Armenia. The latter is the source of a silver tetradrachm minted between 55 BC and 95 BC, the reign of Tigranes I. It would appear that in Roman times, the port (which probably used the natural harbour then existing in the Hoyle Lake) continued to be significant, and it is believed that a Roman road was built from Chester to Meols. Street Hey in Willaston may be one section of this lost road, while the nearby Hargrave Lane is thought to be a continuation. Barker Lane in Greasby may be another section—the lane becomes a hollow way and ends abruptly at a ridge, looking down on Limbo Lane.

Field names and medieval accounts refer to a 'Blake Street,' apparently another Roman road heading towards Monks Ferry and Birkenhead Pool; here a supposed Roman bridge was found when the Pool was converted into docks in 1850. Built of solid oak beams supported by stone piers, it was about a hundred feet long and buried thirty feet deep in the silt.

The Roman port at Meols is thought to predate the legionary fortress at Chester, having played a part in the conquest of the Celtic tribes of Wales. Although it appears to have been a large settlement, Roman Meols does not appear on Claudius Ptolemy's second century AD map of Britain: the writers P. France and J. Emmett identify it as the mysterious *Portus Setantiorum* (Port of the Setantii tribe), which the 2nd century AD cartographer Ptolemy of Alexandria seems to place further up the coast.

The tribal name of the Setantii is connected with the

Celtic name for the Mersey, the Setiae, and the eminent philologist Sir John Rhys also suggest that it was linked with the name Seithenynn, a prince of Cantre'r Gwaelod, the 'Lowland Hundred', whose drunkenness led to the inundation of that legendary land when he forgot to close the sluices that defended it from the sea. A variant version says that a woman left the lid off a well and the well water flooded out, drowning the low-lying land. Although Cantre'r Gwaelod is usually said to have been in Cardigan Bay, and Portus Setantiorum may have been in Lancashire, it is possible that in these legends of Seithenynn we catch echoes of tales originally told about the lost lands of Wirral.

Meols has produced more medieval finds than anywhere in England outside London. Indications of metalworking suggest that by this period the site was now producing its own goods, but almost two hundred medieval coins confirm that it remained a centre of trade. However, just as no Roman maps show Meols, no surviving medieval documents can confirm its status as a market, and there is no evidence that it ever received a charter, unlike Liverpool. Meols is mentioned in *Domesday Book*, but only as a small settlement. Yet hundreds upon hundreds of archaeological finds confirm its importance until the sixteenth century, when the port that had thrived in medieval times succumbed to the same fate as its predecessors.

Meols only regained any significance in the Regency period, during the development of Hoylake, a fashionable watering hole patronised by aristocrats and poets. Meols was divided into two townships consisting mainly of sandhills and marsh; Great Meols, corresponding roughly with modern Meols, and Little Meols, which took up much of what is now Hoylake.

Sandwiched in between was the small fishing village of Hoose, which has since been swallowed up by Hoylake's town centre. After the shoreline retreated by five hundred metres in under a century—and following the silting up of the Hoyle Lake, the natural harbour that had been the basis for the ancient port—the inhabitants of Hoose and Meols had become poverty-stricken and inbred, relying chiefly on wrecking to survive.

In 1846, Reverend Abraham Hume was visiting Hoylake Parsonage when he noticed a Roman brooch on the mantelpiece. Investigation proved that local fishermen found many ancient artefacts on the shore. Over the next few years he publicised these and other finds, culminating in his 1863 book *Ancient Meols*, and began an archaeological gold rush. It is mainly due to Hume's work that we know anything at all of Meols' incredible history.

In 1891, spring tides removed some of the drift sand and for a while revealed Iron Age huts, a village street, and, in the sand, hoofmarks, the marks of cartwheels, and footprints.

The Sea of Monsters

In the spring of 1636, Sir John Bridgeman, Chief Justice of Chester, was riding on his Lent Circuit when he found a strange creature stranded on the Wirral shore. Fifteen yards high, twenty yards and a foot long, it had a lower jawbone that was five yards high and five long.

Its cry could be heard six or seven miles away, and it was "so hideous that none dared come near it for some time," before the locals killed it. It is referred to as a Herring-Hog in the ballad that describes it, and this is a name given to the harbour porpoise (*Phocaena phocaena*), but its description does not correspond with that of any porpoise known to science.

More recently, two sea creatures have been reported numerous times. The first is commonly known as the Hoylake Monster. Shortly after the Second World War it was seen by the crew of a fishing boat eight miles north west of Hilbre. The boat was stationary, and the skipper, Jones, was able to describe it in detail.

It was oval and about 4'6" by 5'6", with a curved back of which about six inches were visible above the water. Its head was a roundish oval and a fin ran along its back while two more fins were visible on either side. It had a long slender neck rising from the water as much as two feet, while sometimes submerging. Its skin was brownish-black but a pale whitish colour on the underside of its neck. Its eyes and nostrils were like those of a horse and its skin was like an elephant's. The report of its sighting occasioned a "nine days' wonder" in the vicinity.

The fishermen of Wales and Cornwall maintain that a sea monster called Morgawr roams the Irish Sea, a creature with a long neck and a greyish green body. In the 1880s a similar sea monster was seen at Llandudno, while fishermen saw what they described as a creature like a snake with eleven humps swimming from the Dee towards Liverpool Bay. Another sea serpent, perhaps the same one, was seen chasing a baby whale off Hilbre in 1901.

In the early eighties two vessels sank in the Irish Sea, the trawler *Celerity*, which vanished completely, and the *Sheralga*, which was been dragged by her nets for ten nautical miles before capsizing. The same day, the *Crimson Dawn* caught something the size of a whale which dragged it through the sea until the net snapped and the thing escaped. Some months later, the *Galvanor* vanished in the same area, and a year late the *Cite D'Aleth* sank, followed by the *Zanto* and the *Exuberant*. Rumour says that the Navy despatched three Polaris submarines to Liverpool Bay to search for a monster said to resemble Nessie.

A completely different creature has been reported on Hilbre itself.

In 1954, thirteen year old Susan Rogers was visiting the island with her older cousin Tina Jones. After an argument, Susan ran away. Tina went looking for, worried that the tide would come in they would be cut off from the mainland. Meanwhile, Susan had hidden in the Lady's Cave. She was looking out to see if Tina was nearby when she heard a noise from behind her and something touched her ankle. Turning, she saw a huge crab, four feet high and six feet wide, which was staring at her with enormous red eyes.

Susan ran away and Tina found her scrambling across the beach, terrified.

This was not the only time the creature was seen at Hilbre, and it, or another of its unknown species, is said to have been washed up on Parkgate Promenade during a storm in the forties.

King's Gap

King's Gap in Hoylake is named after William of Orange, who stayed in Wirral in 1689, before setting sail for Ireland to fight the Battle of the Boyne against the deposed James II. The king himself stayed at Gayton

Hall[7], which belonged to the Gleggs, the only Protestant gentry family in the hundred, while his general the Duke of Schomberg and the army camped at Leasowe and Meols and the fleet was anchored in the Hoyle Lake. Johannes Van Zoelen, one of William's Dutch soldiers, did not get as far as Ireland but is buried at West Kirby.

To quote Anna Sewell:

'Twas on these Downs the Belgian Hero spread
His ardent Legions in auspicious hours,
Ere to Ierne's hostile shores he led
To deathless glory their embattled Powers.

When, like the Conqueror of the Eastern World,
That stemm'd with dauntless breast the Granic flood,
His victor-sword immortal WILLIAM whirl'd,
And Boyne's pale waters dyed with Rebel blood.

The Curst Fisherman: A Tale of the Wirral

It was once the custom on the Wirral coast that if anyone who found a corpse thrown up by the sea, left it to the mercy of the waves rather than get it Christian burial, he would be deemed to have 'incurred eternal opprobrium and obloquy of the most indelible nature', and that 'the avenging spirit of the unburied corpse will ever afterwards through life perseveringly haunt the unhappy man who disregarded the sacred rights of the dead.'

The Curst Fisherman by Egerton Leigh tells a story of a man who offended that custom, and his awful fate:

---

[7] *In Wallasey, it is said he stayed at the Cheshire Cheese.*

I.

TWO *fishermen loved Bessy Blake;*
A comely maid was she;
Her parent's cot was at Hoylake,
Not far from Hilbre,

II.

Two fishermen loved Bessy Blake,
Each other hated sair;
Their names John Stone and William Lake,
But John she favoured mair.

III.

A wild storm swept the Cheshire shore;
John Stone was on the deep;
His boat, alas! was seen no more,
Which Bessy caused to weep.

IV.

Early next morn Will Lake arose,
The waste of sands he sought;
Landwards a sight his life-blood froze,
The flowing billows brought.

V.

His rival's corpse lay stark and stare,
Half swathed in slimy weed!
One hand still clasped a lock of hair,
Grasped in his utmost need.

VI.

'Twas Bessy's: Lake turned grimly then,
And spurned him as he lay,

And watched till the tide ebbed again,
And whirled the corpse away.

VII.

A shrimper by an old wreck sat;
Unseen the deed he viewed.
Soon known by all, when general hate
The miscreant pursued.

VIII.

Shame on the fisherman, who leaves
A corpse the hoarse wave's sport!
Whose winding-sheet the sea-wrack weaves.
And wild gulls scream the mort.

IX.

No peace had William from that hour,
Within, without the door;
His rival's face still seemed to glour,
As when him last he saw.

X.

By Bessy scorned (for she'd been told
Who'd her dead lover spurned),
Avoided by the young and old,
Despised where'er he turned.

XI.

By night, by day, at eve, at morn,
Still, still, those features sad
Gazed on him with that stare forlorn.
At length the wretch went mad.

15
OVERCHURCH

…whence we go by Moreton, and then by Saughall Massie, a very gallant lordship; and leaving Overchurch on our left hand…

Today, the name of Overchurch is most closely linked with the housing estate and junior school of that name, although it is also a parish containing only one village, Upton. As mentioned in the introduction, the name itself is usually translated as "The Church on the Shore," which seems curious since it is some miles from the sea or either estuary. As a village, Overchurch is omitted from *Domesday Book*, but it appears on Christopher Saxton's 1579 map of Cheshire. Inexplicably, it seems to have vanished sometime after Saxton's survey, leaving only its Norman church. Despite being almost three quarters of a mile from Upton, this church remained the only one in the parish until 1813, when it was demolished after storm damage and decades of neglect. Like Holy Cross in Woodchurch and St. Andrews in Lower Bebington, Overchurch had a circular churchyard, which suggests it was originally a pre-Christian centre of worship.

During demolition, a runic stone from the Anglo-Saxon period was discovered in the walls of the later building. The Overchurch rune stone, known traditionally as the Biddan Stone (some say this is the origin of the place name Bidston), is now in the Grosvenor Museum in Chester. It dates from the eighth or ninth century AD.

Despite the pagan connections of the runic alphabet, the stone is of explicitly Christian origin. Its Old English inscription reads

Folcæ arærdon bec[un...
Ge]biddath fote Æthelmun[d],

translating as

The people erected a memorial...
Pray for Æthelmund.

Æthelmund's identity is unknown. An *ealdorman* (chief magistrate of a shire) with the same name lived in Mercia during the reigns of Offa and Coenwulf (757-796 and 796-821), and died in battle against the men of Wessex in 802. Wirral was part of Mercia in the same period; however, Ealdorman Æthelmund's links seem to have been with the southwest Midlands.

The Overchurch Æthelmund's identity is as much of a mystery as the fate of his village. All that remains today are the ruins of the churchyard, deep within a dense, overgrown thicket in woodland near the Upton Bypass.

16

GREASBY

… we pass by Newton, and somewhat beyond that by Greasby, where we hold on nearer the shore…

On Easter Monday, while the children of Birkenhead were rolling eggs down the Bonks, it was customary in Greasby and Frankby to go round the farms for eggs, chanting:

"Please, Mrs Whiteleg,
Be pleased to give us an Easter egg.
If you won't give us an Easter egg
Your hens will lay all addled eggs
And your cocks lay all stones.
One for Peter, two for Paul,
And three for the One who made us all."

17
WEST KIRBY AND HILBRE

...and take with us West Kirby: here in the utmost western nook of this promontory, divided from the land, lies that little barren island called Ilbree, or Hilbree; in which it is said there was sometime a cell of monks, though I scarce believe it; for that kind of people loved warmer seats than this could ever be.

The Lady's Cave

Hilbre is a tidal island at the mouth of the Dee Estuary. Named after an apocryphal Anglo-Saxon saint, Hildeburgh, it was the site of a small cell of monks in the Middle Ages, and according to some stories the destination of a pilgrimage, while in more recent times it was a haunt of smugglers and wreckers. At the time of the Napoleonic War there was an inn on Hilbre, the *Seagull*, whose owner was said to have made his money by wrecking. Hilbre itself is the main island while two other islands, Middle Eye and Little Eye, lie adjacent to it. On the seaward side of Middle Eye is a cave known as the Devil's Hole, where smugglers are said to have kept their contraband.

The main island also has a cave, called the 'Lady's Cave.' A ledge of rock behind it is named the Lady's Shelf. It is a popular spot for tourists and other visitors to the island, though few people know to what dramatic events the name refers.

One evening, so the story tells us, long ago in the Middle Ages, one of the monks who lived on the island came to the cave where he was appalled to see the unmoving form of a maiden lying on the shelf of rock. She wore rich clothes and a carcanet of jewels stood on her black hair. He turned to run back up and seek aid from the other monks when he heard a weak voice from the maiden.

"Stay, father, stay; give me the last rites. My time is short."

The monk returned to the maiden's side, and with her last breath she told him her story….

A knightly pennon floated in the breeze above the turrets of Shotwick Castle. The maiden, whose named was Gertrude, was the daughter of the castellan of the castle, his only child. Her mother had died giving birth to her, and her father had no one else, but Gertrude grew up with his squire Edgar as her closest friend, a brother in all but name.

Edgar was tall and strong, with hair that curled over a broad forehead. He was the first in the hunt, and the first in war. Once he took a merlin from its nest and tamed it for her. Another time he rescued her when her boat was upset in the river. When an outlaw band from the Forest of Wirral ambushed her and carried her off, it was Edgar who followed, slew their chief, and rescued her. When fire raged through the castle one night and the flames licked around Gertrude's bower, it was Edgar who scaled the blazing tower and carried her to safety. He could also sing, play the lyre, and tell stories. They fell in love.

Gertrude's beauty was famed throughout the region. One day a Welsh knight named Llewellyn came to the castle and he asked the castellan for his daughter's hand in marriage. He was wealthy and of noble blood, and the castellan was eager to find his daughter a suitable husband. When he came to Gertrude's bower and told her what he planned, she turned pale. She realised that there was one man with whom she wished to spend her days, but it was not Llewellyn. When she told her father, he was angry but she could not be persuaded, and soon Llewellyn was riding dolefully out across the drawbridge.

One morning, her father said, "Gertrude, put on your best kirtle before the next tide. We'll spend some hours sailing."

Soon they embarked, and their boat flew over the waves. Little did she know what was to be her fate.

As the vessel reached Point of Ayre, her father said, "Gertrude, your fate is sealed. You shall share Llewellyn's bed as his bride. This evening the marriage party meets, and the vassals will throng. It is fitting that the daughter of a knight should marry a knight. You grieve for Edgar in vain, because I have found him a bridal couch he will never leave—the depths of the sea."

She shuddered as he spoke. She did not feel fear, nor did she weep, but she swooned when she heard of

Edgar's death and a sudden surge swept over the boat and she was dragged into the waves.

As she went, she thought she heard her father cry:

"Save my child! Edgar lives! If he's your choice, then he is mine—my child! My child!"

Then the waves bore her off and she knew no more until she awoke in this cave.

"My ebbing pulse foretells my doom," she told the monk. "Strip off each bridal gem; wed my cold body to the tomb, and sing my requiem. Tell Edgar I've been sorely tried, that with my last breath —"

She ceased. The monk looked up and sighed, knowing that this was death.

The Constable Sands

The second Earl of Chester after the Norman Conquest was Richard D'Avranches, son of Hugh Lupus. Shortly after succeeding his father, still very young, he decided to make a pilgrimage to Saint Winifred's Well in North Wales. When the wild Welshmen heard of his coming, they rushed down furiously from the mountains and attacked the Earl, cutting off his retreat to Chester, hoping to kill him or take him hostage. The Earl took refuge in Basingwerk Abbey, and sent a messenger to the Constable of Chester, William fitzNigel, Baron of Halton, asking the constable to raise a great army and meet him there as soon as possible.

On receiving the message, the constable gathered a strong host and they rode fast through Wirral towards Hilbre, trusting that there would be enough ships to convey them all, but when they reached the shore, there were none.

The host made "dolorous grievance and great lamentation... for love and tenderness," knowing their master the Earl was in such dire straits. Some "wept and wailed without consolation, some sighed and sobbed, some were in ecstasy without perfect reason." William fitzNigel consulted a monk who lived on Hilbre as a hermit, and asked him for his advice. The monk told him to kneel and

> *humbly to beseech St. Werburgh his patroness*
> *for help and remedy in such great distress.*

The constable began to pray:

> *Blessed Werburgh and virgin pure,*
> *I beseech thee meekly help me this day,*
> *That we may transcend this river safe and sure,*
> *To save and defend my lord from discomfiture;*
> *And here I promise to God and thee alone,*
> *To offer to thee a gift at my coming home.*

He ended his prayer with tears. Then, just as the Red Sea had split to let Moses and the Jews escape from Egypt, dry sands appeared crossing the river between Hilbre and Basingwerk.

The constable and all the company, seeing this great miracle that transcended nature, praised God and Saint Werburgh. They crossed to Wales on the sands, delivered their lord from his enemies, and brought him safely again to Chester.

William the constable came to the monastery, thanked Saint Werburgh and fulfilled his promise by offering to the place the village of Newton. Later he founded Norton Priory in Cheshire.

Despite this miraculous delivery from death, Earl Richard's life was short: he was drowned alongside the heir to the throne and many of the younger nobles of England in the wreck of the White Ship, a terrible event that resulted in the civil wars of Stephen and Matilda.

The Hilbre Mermaid

A lifeboat man from the lifeboat station on Hilbre was washed over the side as they set out into rough seas.

As his fellow crewmen attempted to haul him back into the boat, he saw a woman in the water not far away. Once he had got back on board, he told the others what he had seen and, assuming she was drowning, asked them to head for the spot where he had seen her. But when they got there, she had vanished. The crew searched the water for her before heading for the vessel they had been called out to save.

When they returned later on, the lifeboat man saw the woman again but this time she upended into the water and he saw the splash of her tail. Then he realised she must be a mermaid.

He told no one about this until many years later when he was on his deathbed. It was his belief that she protected the Hilbre lifeboat men.

Warrior Monks

After the Norman Conquest, much of Wirral belonged to Robert de Rodelent (of Rhuddlan), cousin of Hugh Lupus, the Earl of Chester, both of whom were related to William the Conqueror himself. Robert's fortunes increased and eventually, as vassal of Earl Hugh, he became lord of North Wales after he captured the Welsh king Griffith, who was imprisoned in Chester.

But Griffith was later released by his men and began carrying out piratical raids on Robert's lands. His mother was of Viking stock, and many of his supporters came from his mother's people, the Vikings of Dublin, who also had links with the inhabitants of Wirral. Tradition maintains that the people of Wirral raided the neighbourhood of Chester in league with the Welsh, so perhaps some of these were Robert's rebellious tenants. Some years later, Wirral was turned into a royal hunting forest as a punishment for the unruliness of its inhabitants (see the chapter on Storeton).

Robert was in the midst of his noontide nap in his castle at Deganwy, near the Conwy, when news reached him of raiders come ashore at Great Orme. He sent messages to muster his troops but on discovering that the Welsh, led by Griffith, were about to make a getaway, rushed down to attack them accompanied by only one man, and fell beneath a shower of arrows — none of the Welsh dared fight him hand to hand. They cut off his head and took it back to their ships as a trophy before his men could reach the shore. When his men found his headless body, they took it back to Chester for burial at the abbey of St. Werburgh.

Before his death, he had presented West Kirby and the monastic cell on Hilbre to the monastery of St. Evroul in Normandy. However, the abbot of St. Evroul soon presented the lands to his opposite number at St. Werburgh's Abbey in Chester, in return for an annual payment of thirty shillings. Somehow, by the reign of King Stephen, the lands had come into the possession of the fourth Earl of Chester, Ranulf de Gernones, who bestowed them upon the monks of Basingwerk Abbey, on the Welsh coast.

The monks of St. Werburgh questioned the Earl's right to give the lands to Basingwerk, but the latter monastery held them from 1154 until 1200. The dispute came to a head during a meeting between the monks of Basingwerk and those of Chester in the churchyard of St. Bridget's, the parish church in West Kirby. By now, it seems, the Earl of Chester supported the St. Werburgh's claim, which was being made by Thomas of Capenhurst, the current abbot. The current earl was another Ranulf, Ranulf de Blundeville, who later distinguished himself as a Crusader and became the focus for a series of ballads that in the fourteenth century were once as popular as the tales of Robin Hood. Perhaps due to his presence at the meeting, it degenerated into an armed combat.

The results of this meeting of warrior monks are unrecorded, but fifteen years later, the next appointment was made by the Abbot of St. Werburgh's.

Tell's Tower

A little to the south of the Marine Lake in West Kirby, now concealed behind more recent developments, is a small round tower of sandstone known as Tell's Tower. It commemorates Tell, a St. Bernard dog (or German Shepherd, according to some stories) who died in the late nineteenth century while rescuing his master, the Reverend Cumming McDona MP, who lived in Hilbre House (since demolished).

On the night of January 22, 1871, MacDona found himself in difficulty while swimming out on the Irish Sea. Seeing that his master was drowning, Tell swam far out into the sea, grabbed MacDona from the waves and carried him all the way back to the shore. With his master safely back home, the dog lay down, exhausted, on the sand, and died.

At the tower's base is an inscription that records the dog's heroism, alongside a carving of Tell. The dog himself is buried beneath it.

During the Second World War, the tower was used as a lookout post while Hilbre House later became the home of Selwyn Lloyd, Speaker of the House of Commons. Since the house was demolished, the erection of new houses has made access to Tell's Tower impossible.

William and Mary

A folk song collected in the 1960s from 'the late Mr. Hale of West Kirby' tells the story of William and Mary, two lovers who are parted when William has to go away—presumably to seek his fortune, although the song does not make this clear. They promise to be true, but Mary hears nothing from him for three years before a one-eyed beggar approaches her at her door and she asks for news of William. It transpires that this is William in disguise, testing her love for him, and at the conclusion of the song, he promises to whisk her away to the church "e'er the sun sets" to marry her.

Customs and Traditions

Of old, West Kirby was noted for its ghosts. One haunted the narrowest part of the lane between West Kirby and Caldy, while the ghost of Mrs Glegg, a former lady of the manor, was said to walk abroad at night on the Mount (the part of Caldy Hill near Kirby Mount). The most feared ghost was "he who walked in Highfield

Lane... nobody was bold enough to encounter him when darkness set in..."

A popular belief among nineteenth century schoolboys in West Kirby was that it was of vital importance to spit upon a rock known as the Cat's Face. During Lent, the boys had to attend a service at St. Bridget's, but if they alone were present the service was brief and there was no sermon. If adults attended, however, the service was as long as usual and a sermon was included. Spitting on the Cat's Face would ensure that adults stayed away, including "certain Miss Browns" who frequently attended church services. Should they appear, the boys knew that one of them had failed to make the traditional offering.

Church Customs

Various superstitions and customs were linked with local churches. For instance, it was believed that the spirit of the last person buried in the graveyard remained at the lych-gate and ushered new arrivals to their grave. The belief sometimes resulted in fights when more than one burial happened on a day, each side wanting to bury its dead first so it would be conveyed to the grave by the ghost. It was also seen as a bad omen for a bride and groom to pass through the lych-gates.

It was held to be particularly unlucky for a burial to take place on the north side of a church. This came from a belief that the northern part was for the burial of unbaptized children, excommunicated people, and suicides. It was also where the bodies of strangers drowned during shipwrecks were buried, something that was seen as the duty of anyone who found a body on the shore; should they fail in this duty, the ghost of the drowned person would haunt them, which is the theme of Egerton Leigh's previously quoted poem *The Curst Fisherman*. At St. Bridget's, a special bier was kept at the church for the purpose, and the road to the shore was nicknamed "Corpse Alley," since it was the way taken by the bier. Drowned corpses were a common occurrence on the shore, sometimes due to the nefarious activities of wreckers.

Another belief relating to funerals was that anywhere a coffin had been carried automatically became a right-of-way, a notion that was exploited unsuccessfully by the customs men on one occasion, who tried to have a coffin taken through Mother Redcap's so they could gain easy access to the notorious smugglers' tavern (see the chapter on Wallasey).

Despite these gloomy customs and superstitions, churchyards were also the venue for games, dances and fairs. Cock-fighting, singlestick and wrestling matches went on after Evensong. Another custom was the Church Ale, where the churchwardens brewed a "considerable quantity" of strong ale, which was sold in order to raise funds for the church building.

Another custom was rush-bearing. Rushes were used widely as a floor-covering before carpets became widely available, and the rushes for the church were carried in decorated harvest-wagons, drawn by the village's best horses. The wagons were covered with flowers and ribbons, with the rushes stacked in them as high as possible, kept in place by "harvest gearing," rails made of wood that were hidden by coloured paper cut into decorated patterns, just as the ropes that kept the rushes in place were covered in flowers. The floor of St. Bridget's was strewn with rushes until 1758, and the ceremony was celebrated every year, but came to an end when the floor was replaced with flagstones.

18
FRANKBY

From thence we come next to the Graunge, which I would rather think to be that seat where those monks eat their beef and brewis, and which is now possessed by William Glegg, esquire, being descended to him from his ancestors; upon the side of this to the east lies Frankley (Frankby), a large township.

Frankby had a Mummers' Play at Christmas, and the mummers went round to kitchens, inn parlours and the houses of the gentry until 1937. The play went as follows:

Characters
Little Wit—Red pants and tails, top hat and big bow-tie
King George—old red military tunic, blue pants with red stripe down side; wooden sword, helmet
Bold Slasher—khaki uniform with wooden sword,

helmet

Doctor Brown—tails, top hat, large portmanteau full of bottles etc.

Beelzebub—old man with beard and hump on back: old hat: carrying dripping-tin. Long tail of plaited straw stiffened with a wire.

All have blackened faces.

Enter LITTLE WIT

In comes I that's never been yet
With my big head and little wit.
Although my wit is very small,
I'll do my best to please you all.
Stir up that fire and give us a light
For in this house there'll be a fight.
If you don't believe in what I say
Step in King George and clear the way.

Enter KING GEORGE

In comes I King George, the noble champion bold.

It was me that fought the fiery dragon and won £10, 000 in gold.

It was me that followed the fair lady to the giant's gate.

The giant he almost struck me dead.

I drew my broad and trusty sword

And nearly cut off his head.

BOLD SLASHER shouts from outside.

Ha! Ha!! and enters.

The valiant soldier, Bold Slasher, is my name,

If I was to draw my broad and trusty sword, I'd surely win their game.

KG How canst thou win the game
When my head is made of iron;
My body's made of steel;
My hands and feet are

Made of knuckle-bone?
I'll challenge thee to fight.
BS *Put out thy purse and pay.*
KG *Pull out thy sword and slay,*
Or else we'll have a recompense
Before we go away.
BS *Right.*

Both start to fight. KG stabs BS, who falls.

LITTLE WIT (shouts) *Doctor! Doctor!*

DOCTOR BROWN (shouts from outside) *No doctor to be found.*

LW *Ten pounds for a doctor.*

DOCTOR BROWN enters:

In comes I, Doctor Brown,
The best doctor in the town.
LW *How came you to be a doctor?*
DB *By my travels.*
LW *Where did you travel?*
DB *Hickity, Dickity, France and Spain,*
Back to Old England to cure the man that lives in the lane.
LW *How much will you cure this man for?*
DB *Ten pounds.*
LW *No less?*
DB (feeling BD pulse) *Nine,*
And a bottle of wine.
LW *Cure him.*

Doctor opens portmanteau, takes out several bottles and mixes a concoction:

Now, Jack, open thy throttle,
Take three drops from this bottle.
Rise up, Bold Slasher, and fight a battle.

BS rises up and starts to fight KG.

LW *Put up thy swords and be at rest,*
For peace and quietness is the best.

BEELZEBUB enters:

In comes I, old Beelzebub,
On my back I carry a knob,
Under my arm I've a dripping pan.
I think myself a jolly old man.
I court the lassies plenty.
One by one and two by two;
But there's none to come up to my fancy.
I've a little tin under my arm.
A copper or two will do it no harm;
A shilling or two will do it some good,
Please, ladies and gentlemen, put something in good.

19

THURSTASTON

...and so we come to the two townships Great and Little Caldy.

Near unto which lies the station or landing place for their boats and barges, with their laden and unladen commodities, called the Red-bank; so I take it from the colour of the rock upon the shore-brink; and near unto this lies Irby, another fair lordship, wherein the Balls, freeholders, have a good seat. And we come thence to Thurstanton, the ancient seat of the Whitmores of Thurstanton, the owner now Whitmore, esquire; which race, whether they had their beginning from the city of Chester, in which have been many mayors of that name, or that from them came the name into Chester, their own evidence, wherewithal I am not acquainted, can better declare it than I can.

Thor's Stone

Thor's Stone (also known as Thor's Rock, Red Rocks, and Rockley's, among others) is on Thurstaston Common, a massive block of sandstone that sits in a natural amphitheatre, surrounded by wood and heathland. According to local legend, this 'gigantic rock altar' was the site of Viking religious rites in honour of the thunder god Thor—the red rock is stained with the blood of victims!—or else, was raised by the Vikings to commemorate the Battle of Brunanburh; or, was held to be sacred to Thor after lightning was seen striking the rock; or in a tradition recorded by Professor Steve Harding in *Ingimund's Saga*, it is the location of Thor's Hammer, the weapon the Norse god uses to fight the frost giants. But is there truth in any of these stories?

No, would appear to be the short answer. Writing in *Notes & Queries* in November 1877, local worthy Sir James Picton brought to the attention of the general populace the 'Great Stone of Thor' a 'very interesting relic of Saxon or Danish heathendom.' Stating that there was no local legend about it, and that local historians did not mention it, he linked the rock with the township in which it was located, suggesting that it was 'Thor's Stone,' and that the name Thurstaston came from *Thors-stane-tun*, or the town of Thor's Stone. His real agenda was to stop the encroachment of developers in the area, and the article is directly responsible for Thurstaston Common becoming a public park rather than a Victorian housing development.

Regardless of this, the story grew and grew. The associations between Thor's Stone and pre-Christian religion were such that in the late nineteen eighties, members of an organisation called the Hearth of the

Sons of Odin provoked a minor furore when they 'reclaimed' the rock for the worship of Thor and other Norse gods. Spoilsport academics maintain that the association is bogus: 'Thurstaston' actually derives from *Thorsteins tun*, or "the farm of Thorstein," Thorstein being a popular name in the Viking Age. So the myth has been debunked. Thor's Stone, despite its symbolic status relating to Wirral's Viking heritage, had no pagan connections prior to 1989. Various theories have been advanced to explain the existence of the rock outcrop, including the possibility that it was part of a quarry, perhaps the site of a crane for loading stone into carts. However, no records exist of such a quarry and it is worth pointing out that, although Thorstein was indeed a Norse personal name, it means 'Thor-stone.'

The *Journal of the British Archaeological Association*, Vol. XLIV, printed in 1888, included an article describing a trip made by its members to Wirral, during which they visited 'the Thor Stone' where Picton himself regaled them with its supposed history. Again, he maintained that no legend was associated with the area (clearly unaware that he had invented one) but he was corrected by the Reverend A. E. P. Gray, Rector of Wallasey, who said that

...the people round about the country gave the name of "Fair Maidens' Hall" to the place where the Stone stood, and ... the children were in the habit of coming once a year to dance round the Stone...

Obscure folkloric rites such as these are often held to represent traditions dating back to pagan antiquity. Perhaps no one prior to Picton had linked the rock with the mighty Thunderer of Norse religion, but this picturesque area was certainly the centre of earlier traditions.

Other legends tell of covens of witches at large in the area, and even a human sacrifice cult centring on the worship of a pagan cat-god known as the Moggan Tar.

Another source of evidence for paganism in Wirral is to be found in place names and field names containing the element 'harrow.' This derives from the Old English *hearg*, meaning a pagan shrine, related to the Old Norse *hörg*. A *harrowe hay* was recorded in Heswall in 1293, while a whole crop of 'harrow' field names is to be found not far from the apocryphal Thor's Stone.

First mentioned in two academic articles published in 1993, Harrow Fields lie between Oldfield and Thurstaston, on either side of Telegraph Road. A field-walking expedition carried out a year earlier by Rob Philpott of Liverpool University yielded many archaeological relics suggesting occupation of the area from prehistory until the Viking Age. Linking the field names with the long period during which the site was occupied, Sarah Semple of Durham University concluded that this area was the scene of pre-Christian religious ritual in the Viking Age, the Saxon period, during the Roman occupation, and throughout the Iron and Bronze Ages, the New Stone Age and all the way back to the Middle Stone Age, between 9000 and 7000 years ago. Dr Semple maintains that this theory is reinforced by the continuity of religious and ritual connections with the area: not only the close proximity of Thurstaston Rectory, but also the fact that to the present day, Thurstaston Common continues to be the focus for 'low-level ritual activity.'

Perhaps Sir James Picton wasn't so wrong after all.

Thurstaston Hall

Thurstaston Hall has several legends. One tells of the wooden figure that stands in a niche on the staircase. It is said to represent Hugh Lupus, the first Norman Earl of Chester. Tradition says that this was once stolen but recovered from the Dee.

Another story says that there is a passage or tunnel that leads from the cellar to the banks of Dawpool Deep, somewhere in the vicinity of Caldy Sailing Club. The existence of this legendary tunnel was apparently confirmed in August 1971, when Water Board workers laying new pipes for a private road off Station Road in Thurstaston stumbled upon what appeared to be a smugglers' tunnel running from the direction of the manor house towards another house in the village, or possibly in the direction of the lost port of Dawpool.

According to Ted Weston, who was one of the workers' colleagues, they were jackhammering when they went through the road surface, uncovering part of the tunnel. Sylvia Turner, daughter of Colonel Turner, the owner of the manor house, went down the narrow passage for some distance. It was scattered with infall, but she noticed that there were seats along the wall at short distances. Speculation was rife as to its original purpose, but the two most popular theories were that it had been an underground route for escaping priests during the Reformation, or that it was a smugglers' tunnel. Mr Weston also told the author that traditions of tunnels had already existed in the area, with stories in Irby of a tunnel leading from what is now the Irby Club (formerly the Rookery) to Irby Hall, and a second passage leading from the moat surrounding Irby Hall to Thurstaston Hall.

The Ghost of Thurstaston Hall

Many years ago, a famous and successful portrait painter, Mr W. Easton of the Royal Academy, was staying at Thurstaston Hall while painting a portrait of the family then at the hall. He had been given the arch room in the west wing, a vaulted room that formed part of the old chapel.

Easton had been sleeping in this room, in a magnificent four-poster, for some time without experiencing anything untoward.

One morning in the small hours he heard the door to the room open and he looked up to see an old woman wringing her hands, apparently in great distress. She stood at the foot of his bed and said nothing, even when he said, "You seem to be in great trouble! Is there anything I can do for you?"

She went to the other side of the room, pulled a bell-rope, and disappeared.

The same happened the following night, and so many times that, although he could only believe it to be a supernatural experience, he lost any feeling of fear, to the extent of drawing a rough sketch of the apparition.

A while later a man who knew this story and had seen the sketch was staying at a house somewhere else in England. He recognised one of the family portraits as identical to the apparition in the sketch.

When he asked the family about it, they told him that they had once occupied Thurstaston Hall, and the lady in the painting was the former lady of manor who was said to haunt the place, having killed her own child with a knife which she dropped on being disturbed. When one of her servants finally found the knife, she was put on trial and executed, but her ghost continues to search for the murder weapon.

When the man mentioned this to Easton, he swore that he had never heard of the family, or their legend, and had certainly never seen the portrait.

A photograph of the sketch recently sold on EBay for over four hundred dollars.

The Haselwall Legacy

A feud raged for generations between the Whitmores (owners of Thurstaston and the surrounding lands), and the Vernon family of Shipbrook, one of the seven baronial families of Cheshire. Sir William Stanley, master forester (see the chapter on Storeton), and his younger brother John accompanied Ralph de Vernon in a raid on Thurstaston. To understand why the Baron of Shipbrook led an unruly posse of dissolute Cheshire nobles in an attack on Thurstaston Hall, it will be necessary to step back further in time...

King Edward I visited Wirral in 1277 while preparing for his attack on North Wales. A few years earlier, when Edward had returned from the crusades to take his throne, he had summoned Llewellyn ap Griffith, Prince of Gwynedd, to do homage to him as his overlord. This was a direct challenge to Prince Llewellyn, whose dynasty had been resisting the English for centuries. As the independent ruler of his own principality, Llewellyn refused.

Edward raised an army of one thousand knights and fifteen thousand foot soldiers. He invaded Wales from Wirral, sailing from Shotwick Castle across to Flint, where he began work on Flint Castle, first in a programme of castle-building that was to result in a circle of fortifications; Rhuddlan, Conway and numerous others, ringing Llewellyn's mountainous domain. After cutting Llewellyn off from Anglesey, the "mother of Wales," from which the Welsh got most of their grain, Edward forced the Prince to surrender and accept him as overlord.

During this period, Haselwall, or Heswall as it is today, was home to a man named Patrick. Little is known of him at this point, although it is believed that he was born around 1230, making him in his late forties at the time of the Welsh war. He joined King Edward on his campaigns in North Wales, and in return for his services he was made a knight. As a result, he came to own lands in Heswall, Thurstaston, Great Caldy, and also held half the manor of Speke. To top it all, he became Sheriff of Cheshire. Although history does not record them, his services to his king in the Welsh wars must have been substantial to deserve such a lavish reward.

Sir Patrick had two sons and three daughters by his wife, Agnes de Thurstanston, who he married in about 1290, gaining lands in Thurstaston to which she was heiress. Sir Patrick's eldest son, David, married Eustachia, daughter of Ralph de Vernon, Baron of Shipbrook[8]. After his nephew Warine died while fighting in France, Ralph, who was Rector of Hanwell, had pursued a long legal feud against his nieces, seizing half the Shipbrook estates in the process. Ignoring his vows of celibacy, taken on entering the priesthood, Ralph fathered Eustachia and two sons, including his namesake. Ralph de Vernon the Younger, in his old age (he is said to have lived for a hundred and fifty years and gained the nickname 'Long Liver'), proved even more unscrupulous than his father.

David de Haselwall and Eustachia had five sons and one daughter, Cecily, who received Thurstaston as her dowry. At the age of sixteen, she married John de Whitmore, and Thurstaston passed into the hands of the Whitmores, a family originally from Staffordshire. However, the Whitmore claim to the legacy of Sir Patrick de Haselwall was not to go uncontested.

Ralph de Vernon (the Younger) seems to have coveted his sister's estates. It had been settled that Thurstaston should pass to Cecily and her husband, or in default to Ralph's brother, Richard. When Cecily and John de Whitmore succeeded, Ralph plotted against them. Like his father before him, Ralph began his

---

[8] *Now Shipbrook Hill Farm near Northwich.*

campaign with lawsuits, claiming that Thurstaston had been seized unlawfully from "a certain Alice... [in]... time of peace" during King Edward I's reign, and that the Haselwall claim was thus invalid. Sir Patrick had in fact received the manor as his wife Agnes' dowry. Agnes was daughter of Peter de Thurstanston, whose claim to the manor could be traced back to Robert of Rhuddlan, who received Thurstaston, and numerous estates in Wirral and elsewhere, following the Norman Conquest.

Ralph de Vernon's trumped-up claims proved unsuccessful in court. By now very old, he turned to other means of ensuring his brother gained Thurstaston, and entered into a criminal conspiracy with Sir William Stanley and his brother John Stanley. What they stood to gain is unknown, but it is recorded that they and their men accompanied Ralph de Vernon to Thurstaston, armed with bows and arrows: during this period, Cheshire archers were renowned both for their skill and their lawlessness. On surrounding the hall Ralph de Vernon and his cronies were challenged by a woman inside. During the ensuing altercation, they told her to go and call a bailiff to settle the matter. When she departed, they forced their way into the hall and closed the door behind them. The manor was theirs.

The conclusion to this saga of Cheshire gentlemen gone bad is less dramatic. Forced to give up the hall, the Stanleys and their ally were put on trial for trespass and forced entry, despite their rank. Ralph de Vernon never got Thurstaston, which remained in the possession of the Whitmores until the mid-eighteenth century. On the other hand, the Vernon family line died out in 1403, when Ralph's grandson Richard was executed for treason after fighting on the wrong side at the Battle of Shrewsbury.

Customs of Thurstaston

In the late 1890s, Easter was celebrated in Thurstaston, as it was elsewhere, with "pace-egging." A team of five went from house to house, four of them dressed as the characters mentioned in the verses they sang. They included a boy in female clothes as the Lady, and old Tosspot dressed as a tramp. The verses went as follows:

Here come five hearty lads all of one mind.
We've come a-paste-egging if you will prove kind:
If you will prove kind and never will fail,
We'll treat our young lassies to the best of X ale.
Fol di-diddle dol-di-day.

The next that steps in is Lord Nelson, you see,
With a bunch of blue ribands tied on to his knee;
With a star on his breast live silver doth show,
And he comes a-paste-egging with his jolly crew.
Fol di-diddle…

The next that steps in is the jolly Jack-tar
Who sailed with Lord Nelson during the war,
And has now come ashore Old England to view
And has come a-paste-egging with a juvenile crew.
Fol di-diddle…

The next that steps in is a Lady so gay
Who from her own country has run far away,
With red cap and feathers that look very fine,
And all her delight is in drinking red wine.
Fol di-diddle…

The next that comes in is old Tosspot, you see,
He's a valiant old fellow in every degree,
He's a valiant old fellow and wears a pig-tail
And all his delight is in drinking mulled ale.
Fol di-diddle…

The Master and the Mistress that sit by the fire
Put your hand in your pocket, that's all we desire.
Put your hand in your pocket and pull out your purse.
And give us a trifle, you'll ne'er be the worse.
Fol di-diddle…

Some eggs and fat bacon we'll never deny,
For the eggs we can suck while the bacon doth fry.
Now all ye young lassies mind what you're about
If you give naught we'll take nought, so we'll bid you good night.
Fol did-diddle….

20

BARNSTON

On the east side of it lies Barnston, whence it is like the Barnstons, gentlemen in Broxton hundred, had their own name first...

The Barnston Dale Fiddler

In Barnston Dale, when New Year's Eve coincides with the full moon, there appears in the dale a ghost known as the Phantom Fiddler. Tradition says that the sound of fiddle-playing can be heard all along the dale, and that anyone who sees the ghost risks bad luck, madness, or even death.

The story [9]goes that in 1952, a boy dared his older brother and his sister-in-law to go down into Barnston

---

[9] *Recorded on www.sufferingsmoke.com*

Dale that New Year's Eve, there being a full moon that night. They accepted the dare and walked the mile from his family's house to the dale. It had been snowing earlier and as they set out the snow began again.

They walked along Barnston Road towards the stretch where it goes down into the dale, passing a house on the left. It was then that they saw a figure about fifty yards ahead, walking in the same direction. They thought it was a man wearing a greatcoat, and it stood out clearly against the drifts of snow. The man wanted to call out to the stranger but his wife was scared and stopped him. It looked to her as if the figure had no head.

When they reached the spot where they had first seen the man, they were surprised to find that he had left no footprints. There were none on the pavement at all apart from their own, and the snow was not so thick as to cover them. The figure still walked ahead of them, going down the road into the dale. The couple could not explain it, and they hurried home without taking up the dare.

The next time that the full moon will coincide with New Year's Eve is 2017.

The Battle of Barnston Dale

Legends tell of a battle in Barnston Dale; in some versions between Roundheads and Cavaliers during the Civil War, in others, back in Viking times. It seems that the origin of the legends is Nicholas Size's 1933 book, *Ola The Russian*, which tells the story of Olaf Trygvasson, the Viking king who converted Norway to Christianity with fire and the sword in the late tenth century. During his years of exile, he came to England, where a hermit on the Scilly Isles converted him. In Size's embellished account, events recorded in the sagas are located in Viking Wirral, including *Chapter Twelve — The Great Fight In Barnston Vale*. It seems that the author thought 'vale' was more romantic than 'dale', although this is ironic since the latter is in origin a Norse word.

Size relates how Wirral and all the Viking colonies along the Irish Sea coast from Cumberland to Flint had previously been ruled by Earl Harald, and were now under the control of his widow, Lady Gyda, sister of Olaf Cuaran, king of Dublin. "One of Odin's sacred ravens," Size goes on to say, "running along the surface of the sea, had led the [Viking] colonists to the Mersey in a fog…" They had taken Wirral as their stronghold, and here hd set up their "Thingvalla", i.e, Thingwall, as "a sacred home of justice and liberty…" In a footnote, the author goes on to explain that the earliest depictions of the famous Liver Bird show "a black raven running on the surface of the water."

However, Lady Gyda's claim to rule is contested by Alfin Sigtricson of Litherland, another descendant of the Viking colonists from over the Water, who had established his own Viking parliament at what was later to become Thingwall House in Knotty Ash. The hero of the novel, Olaf, springs to the lady's defence and he and his men defeat Alfin Sigtrygson's warriors in Barnston Dale.

21

HESWALL

...and upon the shore side we come next to the Oldfield, where we said the narrowest place of the hundred is supposed; and it is like hath given name to these gentlemen, the Oldfields, of whom mention has been made before.

Our next remove is to Heswall, or Hesselwall, a town where stand the parish church and parsonage, finely situated; and there extends to it a fair lordship of Thornton Mayow, and Raby, another very pleasant view of a large precinct.

The Hazel Well

The Hazel Well, or Hessle Well, gave its name to Heswall. Its place was marked by a tablet in the wall beside Wallrake, in the Lower Village, on which were engraved the words:

SITE OF
THE HESSLE WELLE.

CLOSED BY PERMISSION
OF THE
WIRRAL HIGHWAY BOARD
1891

It is said that during dry weather fifteen steps led down to the well. In particularly wet weather, however, it overflowed and ran down into what was then the village square, creating an impromptu duck pond. After working in the fields, horses were sent to drink from the well and would return home of their own accord.

It may not be a coincidence that in Celtic myth, the Salmon of Knowledge lives in a well surrounded by hazels, until caught, cooked and eaten by the hero Finn MacCool, who, as a result, gained its wisdom.

Heswall's Buggens

If local tradition is to be believed, ghosts were a common sight in many parts of Heswall; legends that were either exploited or even concocted by smugglers to cover their unlawful operations. When there was to be a landing of contraband on Heswall Shore, it was said that "the ghost walks tonight," the idea being that those who were not in the know would be frightened off.

Other supposedly haunted areas included Barnston Common, (now Whitfield Common and its vicinity), where a headless dog was supposed to roam; the Beacons, which was haunted by a large black hound; the Dales, which was home to a green ghost; Cottage Lane and Well Lane, where the Devil drove his black hearse at night; and the Bloody Gutter on Heswall Shore, where the ghosts of two mariners, who had fought each other to the death over smuggled goods, haunted a path leading to the shore from Broad Lane where the

Dungeon Brook reaches the beach.

Whitfield Common, the Beacons and the Dales remain wild, largely unspoilt areas in a sea of later development. In the eighteenth and early nineteenth century they were only part of the five hundred or more acres of heath that was Heswall Common, perfect country for smugglers to congregate and to store their goods before transporting them on to the purchaser.

These were superstitious times. The stories of ghosts were no doubt told and retold in the inns and alehouses of the area, expanded and elaborated upon until the more fearful villager would never dare go near these locations after dark: even if anyone happened to pass that way when smugglers were abroad, sightings could easily be explained away as ghosts.

Customs of Heswall

An Easter custom was "lifting," which took place on Easter Monday and Tuesday, with men lifting women on the first day, and women lifting men the next. The lifters would go from house to house and, unless given money, they would place the offending person in a chair, or the crossed hands of the lifters, and threw them upwards several times.

The lifters would meet in the village square, at the White Lion Inn on the corner of Wallrake, now White Lodge, a private house. They would choose themselves a leader, place him on horseback and parade him round the village.

In 1833 three men came to a house in Heswall with the intention of lifting the housewife. Her husband was unimpressed and brought a case against the three men before the magistrates of Neston. The men's plea was that this was an old Cheshire custom, which they had a perfect right to follow, and the case was dismissed.

On Shrove Tuesday, schools had a half day holiday, referred to in the popular rhyme:

Pon-cake deay is a very 'appy deay'.
If you don't give us 'all-deays we'll aw run away.'

As they left the school, they received oranges, provided by a shop in the village. Then they would play a game where they had to hit an object with sticks, the winner of the game being rewarded with gingerbread.

In Heswall, May 29th, what was elsewhere known as Oak Apple Day (celebrating the Restoration of the Stuart monarchs), was Nettling Day. Any child who did not wear a spring of oak symbolising loyalty to the throne, was thrashed with nettles by other children.

22
GAYTON

But near the sea side we come to Gayton, the seat of that ancient race of Gleggs of Gayton, now the possession of Edward Glegg, esquire, a gentleman well reputed...

Near Gayton Hall is the Pin Well, which required a pin to be dropped into it before granting a wish. William of Orange's horses are said to have drunk from this well while the king was staying at nearby Gayton Hall, before he set sail (from King's Gap: see the chapter on Hoylake), for Ireland and the war with James II that ended with William's victory the Battle of the Boyne.

Another tradition concerns the Gayton Wishing Well, on Gayton Lane. According to one tradition, "anyone who may here form a wish, and throw a stone backwards into the well will ensure the realisation of their desires." Egerton Leigh was inspired to pen the following:

I.

THE Wishing Well, the Wishing Well
In Gayton lane you find;
Oft had I of the spring heard tell,
Sought by fond maid or hind.

II.

Should ought fair maiden long to have,
She flies to this lone spot;
She throws a stone into the wave,
Then seeks again her cot.

III.

She fancies as the bubbles rise
Above the sinking stone,
Her wish must realise the prize
For which she left her home.

IV.

Look under that rock moss-grown cope
That roofs the Wishing Well;
For there each pebble speaks of hope,
Of hundreds heaped pell-mell.

V.

And none of those who fling a stone,
And breathe fond wishes here,
But deem they thus the seeds have sown
Of fruit esteemed most dear.

VI.

Young Nelly trusts that from the fair
To which her Lubin's gone,

He may bring back to deck her hair
Some gaud — she drops a stone.

VII.

When he that e'en returns to Nell,
And brings the sighed-for toy,
She's sure to stone and Wishing Well
She owes her simple joy.

VIII.

Too oft we think we victims are
Of disappointments chill.
That we alone (poor martyrs) bear
The brunt of every ill.

IX.

But could we register and note
Our granted wishes all,
Soon, soon, our discontent, I wot,
Like blighted fruit would fall.

X.

As I thought thus and mused beside
The Gayton Wishing Well
I fancied on the wall I spied
A strange fern in its cell.

XI.

I tore the treasure from its nook;
When I gazed on it near,
I cried (triumphant at my luck),
More than I wished is here.

XII.

Thus, through life's journey we may share
The long-sought wish, and more.
Unlooked-for joys than granted prayer,
Are sometimes brighter far.

Gayton Wake

In earlier days, 'wakes' were not connected with funerals but were festivals, usually held once a year. Gayton's wake was so famous that in 1804 it was the subject of a long poem by a Welsh poet, Richard Llwyd, *Gayton Wake, or Mary Dod*, which describes a very fat woman who sold cakes in Chester, and her visit to the fair. Part of it is quoted in the appendices.

Dancing booths were available, and there were pipers, fiddlers, dwarfs and giants, a "learned pig," a dancing bear, and a stone eater. It also included races for men, women, ponies and dogs, a jumping match, catching a pig by the tail after it had been shaved of its bristles and soaped; bobbing for apples in ale; eating a quart of hasty pudding; and "grinning through a horse collar."[10]

---

[10] *More commonly known today as gurning.*

23
NESTON AND PARKGATE

...and next unto lies Leighton, in which is seated in a very ancient house and fine desmesne, another branch of the Whitmores, of a very great descent, the owner now William Whitmore, esquire. And next neighbour to this are the well-known town, parish church and port of Great Neston; and the usual place where our passengers into Ireland do so often lie waiting the leisure of the winds, which makes many people better acquainted with this place than they desire to be, though here be wanting no convenient entertainment, if no other wants be in the way; and here is the station of the ships called The New Key, where they embark and disembark both men, horses, kine and all other commodities on the back of this Neston...

Neston and Parkgate's Buggens

As previously mentioned, ghosts were known as "buggens", and the word remains to this day in Buggen

Lane, which leads from Moorside in Parkgate towards the centre of Neston. One story to explain the name says that a woman lived at Townfield, the house at the top of Buggen Lane, with two young children. One day the children sneaked down to Parkgate for a swim but sadly were drowned. The lane is haunted by the ghost of their mother, still searching for her lost children.

In the late nineteenth century, an artist named Henry Melling lived at the old Quay House near Parkgate, with a bed-ridden invalid niece, Clara Payne. An elderly lady wearing a red cloak used to sit quietly by the fire and keep her company. The girl did not find the old woman at all alarming, and when she stopped appearing, Clara missed her greatly. Who she was, no one could say, but it is thought that she was an "earthbound spirit."

Another strange visitor came to St. Winefride's, the Catholic church in Neston, during the lifetime of Teresa Higginson. She was trusted with the keys to the church whenever the priest was away. One morning when he was absent, Teresa saw a strange priest enter the church. He indicated to her without speaking that he wanted to say Mass.

Although she had never seen him before, she prepared the church for the service. Afterwards, he went into the vestry. Shortly after, she followed him to find that the place was empty and there was no sign that anyone had been there for days. When she asked if anyone had seen him leave, she learnt that no one had.

Finally, the Bishop of Shrewsbury was consulted, and he said that the description of the strange visitor was identical to that of a previous parish priest, now dead and buried in the churchyard.

The Dread Wirral Wapentake

A wapentake (from Old Norse *vápnatak* meaning "weapon take," referring the flourishing of weapons at the end of a Thing, or public assembly) was a division of a shire in areas of the country settled by the Vikings, equivalent to a hundred in other counties.

Wirral was a hundred, but due to its Viking connections, it also had a wapentake court based at Neston, which lasted into the nineteenth century, when George III sold it to a private individual. The buyer exploited his privileges to their utmost; he could make official appointments and compel jury service. He could also issues summonses, levy fines or even imprison people, and he used these rights to his personal profit, as did his successors for the next fifty years, when it came into "better hands."

It was finally abolished by an act of parliament in 1856.

Customs of Neston

Nineteenth century Neston had its own version of pace-egging (see chapters on Bidston and Thurstaston), known as Riding the Lord. On Easter Monday morning, a local "hardcase" was paid to ride a donkey from the top of High Street down to Chester Lane while the crowd jeered at him and pelted him with rotten eggs and rubbish. Cock fighting was also popular at this time, and brawling usually ensued.

Lifting (see the chapter on Heswall) also went on in Neston, and was chiefly done by young men. When the women saw them approaching, they rushed into their homes and locked the doors. If the lifters found an open window, they would enter that way, and lift to their hearts' content.

Ladies' Walking Day is held to this day in Neston on the first Thursday in June. It is an annual custom that began with the founding of the Female Friendly Society in 1817 to raise funds by voluntary subscription for the support of "the old, sick, lame, and infirm members thereof." It consists of a procession down the High Street to the parish church, with all members carrying white staves garlanded with flowers collected from their own gardens. At the church, an "appropriate" sermon is preached, and at four the ladies meet to take tea, under strict orders that they should not be "dressed in stuff, painted linen or cotton gowns, on forfeiture of one shilling to the box."

24

WILLASTON

...to the east lies a large tract of heath and commons, and therein a fair lordship called Childer Thornton.

But keeping still our shore we come to Nesse. And next to that more landwards Wollaston, a great breadth of grounds.

The Wirral Stone

In medieval times, Willaston was the main village in the Hundred of Wirral, and it was the main meeting place. The precise spot where the people of the Hundred met is said to have been at the so-called Wirral Stone, the supposed origin of the name Willaston. This is actually three stones standing beside each other where the Willaston road meets the road to Chester. It resembles a mounting block, although it is referred to on an old map as 'the Pissing Stone.'

However, legend insists that this was indeed the

Wirral Stone, although other accounts maintain that the actual Wirral Stone is now buried beneath the road in front of the Red Lion. When still visible, it was a round stone about three feet wide, on which the local children played "jack-stones."

25
PUDDINGTON

And then have we Burton, a pretty town. And a landing place by the side of a great brow of a promontory reaching into the sea, they call it Burton-head; and next to this we come to that gallant lofty seat of Puddington, overlooking the sea, which so far holds on her large breadth unlimited within the mouth of Dee, wherein have continued the race of the Massies, which has been a great name, divided into many branches from that Hamon Massie one of the Earl's barons, and the owner now Sir William Massie, knight, who adds more lustre to the fame of his predecessors, which seat is also beautified with a fine park...

Wirral's Martyr

Like most of Wirral's gentry, the Massey family of Puddington were recusants, adhering to the Old Religion of Roman Catholicism long after the

Reformation. In the late seventeenth century, the family hired a tutor for their children, John Plessington, an ordained Catholic priest. During the Popish Plot scare of 1679–1681, he was hidden in a secret room in a chimney stack at Puddington Old Hall, but he was betrayed and imprisoned in Chester Castle before being hanged, drawn and quartered.

According to legend, all who testified against him came to a bad end: one died in an accident only a few days after Plessington's trial, and another "ended his life miserably in a pig-sty."

In 1929 John Plessington was beatified by the then Pope, Pius XI.

The Rebel's Ride

Naturally, the Masseys were staunch Jacobites, supporting the exiled Catholic king James II, and the claims of the Old Pretender. When Queen Anne died in 1714 and was succeeded by George I of the House of Hanover, James II's son James seized his chance. With the support of loyal Highlanders, he marched into England, finding recruits south of the Border[11]. William Massey of Puddington, elderly head of the family, joined the army of the Old Pretender under General Forster, and they engaged the Hanoverian forces at the battle of Preston.

The Jacobites were defeated and General Forster surrendered, but many of the Jacobites, including Massey himself, secretly fled the town beforehand. Mounted on a good horse, Massey got safely through

---

[11] *The Jacobite rebellions were supposedly prophesised by Robert Nixon, the Palatine Prophet (see chapter on Bebington).*

the enemy lines, then rode on through Ormskirk, skirted Liverpool, and reached the Mersey estuary at Hale.

Here he urged his horse to swim the river. On the other side he continued his ride before reaching his hall, where the horse dropped dead as it entered the inner courtyard.

Massey, almost as exhausted, retired to his bed. He was later arrested and taken to Chester Castle, like John Plessington before him, and he died there a few months afterwards.

26
GREAT SAUGHALL

...a great spacious common, which they vulgarly call Motherless Heath, lies eastward behind this a great way further, at the one side whereof we see Ledsham; and so we come to Shotwich, a little parish church, and near unto it an ancient house that hath belonged to John Hockenhall of Hockenhall, esquire, and so we come to that gallant park called Shotwick-park, where sometimes have been, and yet are remaining, the ruins of a fair castle that stands upon the brink of Dee within the park, in which is also a fine lodge for the habitation of the keepers of the Princess Highnesses deer in that park, and is in the holding of Sir Richard Wilbraham, aforementioned; from whence we come presently to Great Saughall, a fair lordship, and chiefly belonging to His Highness...

The Horned Woman

In Great Saughall is an old farmhouse where lived Mary Davies, the legendary "Horned Woman of Cheshire." Living there during the seventeenth century, this lady grew horns, beginning as an "Excrescence" at the age of twenty eight, after thirty two years "it changed into horns, in shew and substance much like rams' horns, solid and wrinckled, but sadly grieving the old woman, especially upon change of weather." After four years, she shed these horns, but they had been renewed three times by the time of the printing of the pamphlet that describes her, in 1676.

At this time she had "a pair upon her head of six months' growth, and 'tis not without reason believed they will in a short time be bigger than any of the former, for still the latter have exceeded the former in bigness." A portrait of her, and one of her horns, is at the Ashmolean Museum in Oxford; another horn is at the British Museum. Yet another was presented to the King of France. The story goes that these excrescences were the result of wearing too tight a hat. At the age of eighty one, she was exhibited at the *Sign of the Swanne*, near Charing Cross in London.

She is now remembered in the name of the local pub, *The Horned Woman of Saughall.*

27
RETURN TO CHESTER

...and Little Saughall, another fine township, the lands of sundry freeholders there inhabiting; and along by the precincts of them both, lies a place called anciently Kingswood, where now his Highness's tenants have made enclosures, to the great encrease of corn for the benefit of the country.

And next to this lies, first a goodly ancient seat, upon the brow of Dee banks, called Blacon Hall, the name of the whole lordship, the lands of Sir William Norris, knight of the Bath, whom Lancashire hath the most interest in making his chief residence among them, where he hath great possessions; and then adjoineth Crabhall, the desmesne of William Gamul, a prime alderman of the city of Chester, who there hath a most delicate fine house, to retire into at his pleasure, and choice appendants both for pleasure and profit. Round about it we have nothing left but upon our left hand the two Mollingtons, called Banaster and Torrant, a fair lordship, and whereof much of the lands have belonged to the Mordaunts, great knights of Ocley, in Bedfordshire, but now to several purchasers in those parts. And thus we arrive again at the tip of the toe in our description being to come home presently to the famous city again.

The Viking Attack on Chester

The Vikings settled Wirral in the tenth century AD. Viking place names abound in the peninsula, while Welsh and Irish accounts tell us of Ingimund, a Viking from Ireland who led his men to settle in Wirral before extending his ambitions to an attempt at seizing control of Chester. Less familiar are the Chester traditions that associate the Viking attack with the origins of football.

Long before soccer, rugby, or American football, a form of football was played throughout Britain. Sometimes called Shrovetide football, from the festival during which it was played, this was 'a wild, free game for dozens if not hundreds of players' that was noted mainly for its violence. Two sides would struggle to bring a ball to goals that were often several miles apart. It is still played between villages in Derbyshire, and in the town of Alnwick in Northumberland, but in much of the country it was banned long before the current obsession with Health and Safety.

According to contemporary accounts, "Much harm was done" in the football game played in Chester, "some having their bodies bruised and crushed, some their armes, heads, legges broken, some otherwise maimed and in peril of their life…" As a result, it was banned as early as the reign of Henry VIII. However, as we shall soon see, the aggression of the game was as nothing to the barbaric acts that it celebrated.

As already mentioned, the Vikings who settled in

Wirral came, not straight from Scandinavia, but from Ireland. The first Viking raids on Ireland came in 795, when they sacked the monastic settlement on Lambay Island while harrying and pillaging monasteries on the coasts of the British Isles. In the late 830s, a Norwegian leader known as Turgeis became involved in Irish politics, beginning a violent career during which he targeted churches and monasteries, transforming centres such as Armagh and Clonmacnois into pagan temples.

This did not deter some of the Irish from joining his ranks; the renegades who did so were known as the Gall-Gaedhil, and they became notorious for renouncing their Christianity when they threw in their lot with the pagan invaders. If the 'foreigners' were bad, it was said, the Gall-Gaedhil were worse.

During this period, the Vikings founded Dublin and other major Irish cities as bases for their piratical expeditions. Soon after, rivals from Denmark seized Dublin. The Danes fought alongside the Irish until it no longer suited them, then coldly betrayed them, and joined the Norwegian Vikings. When a Norwegian of royal blood named Olaf the White entered Dublin, he was hailed as king of the Danes and Norsemen in Ireland.

Viking supremacy in Ireland continued for approximately fifty years, by which time the descendants of Olaf's brother ruled Dublin. One of their followers was a man named Ingimund. Little is known about Ingimund. He was a Norwegian rather than a Dane; Professor Stephen Harding, author of *Ingimund's Saga*, has speculated that he was one of those Norsemen displaced from Norway when King Harald Finehair united it with 'fire and the sword.' All that is certain is that in 902 he was in Dublin when Cearbhall, King of

Leinster, attacked it and drove out the inhabitants. This was the beginning of a diaspora whose waves reached as far as Iceland in the north and Normandy in the south. Ingimund, who led one fleet of refugees from the burning city, remained on the Irish Sea.

Contemporary Welsh accounts (the *Annales Cambriae* and *Brut y Tywysogion*) record an unsuccessful attack by 'Igmunt' on Maes Osfeilion in the same year. An adaptation of the story of Ingimund follows:

Ingimund's Invasion (adapted from FT Wainwright)

Ingimund and his Norsemen were driven from Dublin and fled across the sea to Wales. Here the Welsh marched against them, and they fought a hard battle on Anglesey. In the end, the Welsh drove Ingimund's men from their lands. Sailing up the coast, the Norsemen beached in northern Mercia, where they contacted Ethelfleda, Lady of the Mercians. Ingimund, weary of war, asked land of the Lady in which his men could settle. Ethelfleda gave him lands in Wirral. Ingimund remained there peacefully for four winters, but when he saw Chester's prosperity, and the good farmland surrounding it, he wanted to seize it.

He called a gathering of the Norsemen at Thingwall, the place of their parliament, and said that since their lands were poor, they should take Chester by storm and possess it with all its wealth and lands. He said, 'Let us beseech them and implore them first, and if we do not get them willingly in this way, let us contest them by force.' The Norse leaders agreed with him and Ingimund went to his house followed by many men.

Although they made their plans in secret, word reached the ears of Ethelfleda that Ingimund meant to seize Chester. On learning this she mustered her forces, filled Chester with warriors, and rebuilt the walls that the Romans had first raised. The Norse army marched to Chester, camping on Hoole Heath. Since they did not get what they wanted by entreaty, they declared battle on a particular day.

A large force with many freemen awaited them in the city. When the men who were in the city saw, from the wall, the army of the Norsemen approaching, they sent messengers to Ethelfleda to ask her advice. She told them to fight just outside the walls, and to leave the city gate wide open. They should also conceal a troop of horsemen inside. Then the strongest of their warriors should make a feigned retreat into the city, and when the vanguard of the Norsemen followed them, the defenders should shut the gate and admit no more, but take captive those inside the city and kill them.

This was all done, and the Mercians slaughtered the Danes and Norsemen, but Ingimund and the other survivors did not abandon the city. Instead they made hurdles, and put posts under them, and mined the wall under their protection.

Lady Ethelfleda sent messengers to the Gall-Gaedhil, the Irishmen accompanying the Norsemen, saying, 'We have come from faithful friends of yours to address you so that you ask the Norsemen what tokens of lands and treasures they would give to those who would betray the city to them. If they accept this, bring them to swear to a place where killing them will be easy; and when they will be swearing by their swords and by their shields, as is their custom, they will lay aside all their missile weapons.'

The Irishmen did this, and the Danes put away their arms. The Irishmen did this to the Danes because they

163

trusted them less than the Norsemen. They killed many of them like this, throwing rocks and large beams down upon them; many were also killed by darts and spears and other missiles.

But the Norsemen remained under the hurdles, still mining the walls. The Mercians and the Irishmen who were among them threw down large rocks to smash the hurdles. The Norsemen placed large posts under the hurdles to keep them up. The Mercians put all the ale and water of the town in cauldrons, boiled them and poured them over the attackers. The Norsemen responded by spreading hides on the hurdles. Then the Mercians let loose all the beehives in the town, so that the Norsemen could not move their legs or hands because of the bees stinging them. Afterwards they abandoned the city.

It was not long before they returned.

Aftermath

A tradition recorded by the Chester monk Matthew Bradshaw[12] mentions a Danish leader called Harold, and a leader of 'Galwedy' named Maucolyn. The Vikings finally retreated when one of their number attempted to plunder the shrine of Saint Werburgh and was driven insane by the saint herself.

Another account from Chester states that the victorious citizens took the severed head of the Danish leader and celebrated their victory by playing with it the first ever game of football. The Guild of Shoemakers and the Guild of Saddlers replayed this ghoulish game every

---

[12] *Who also told the story of the Constable Sands.*

Shrove Tuesday on the Roodee, using a 'ball of wood painted with flowers.' This game of football in Chester is one of the earliest on record.

With its supposed origins in the Viking Age, the Chester football game predates many others and may be the first game ever to be played; the origin of the game. It is perhaps fitting that it was also the first to be banned. As mentioned before, it was prohibited in 1533 because it was so violent; in 1539, it was replaced by a horse race, and horse races have been held on the Roodee (Chester Racecourse) ever since.

Eventually the Vikings settled in Wirral peaceably, and the area around St. Olave's Church in Chester (named after a Viking saint) seems to have formed a Norse enclave before the Norman Conquest. After the Conquest, as said in the chapter on Storeton, the people of Wirral once again troubled the lands around Chester, in league with the Welsh according to tradition, and in reprisal the hundred was put under forest law.

28
WIRRAL IN MEDIEVAL LEGEND

Medieval Wirral was 'the wilderness of Wirral,' appearing in legend as a semi-mythical place with Arthurian connections. Sir Gawain rode through Wirral, and in Celtic legend, King Arthur's knights visited Wirral while aiding Culhwch in his quest to win the hand of the fair Olwen. Yet the legend that seems most closely linked with the peninsula is one that might shed light on Wirral's lost history.

Celtic Legend

The earliest reference to Wirral in medieval legend comes from the collection of tales named *The Mabinogion* by their nineteenth century translator, Lady Charlotte Guest. It appears in the tale of Culhwch and Olwen, preserved in *The Red Book of Hergest*, written about 1400, now kept in the library of Jesus College, Oxford.

The story itself is thought to have been composed much earlier, in the tenth century, and it is held to be one of the earliest surviving prose tales of King Arthur. It tells the story of young Culhwch, a cousin of Arthur, who asks the king for aid in his attempt to win the hand of Olwen, daughter of chief giant Yspaddaden. Arthur agrees, and sends his best men to aid the youth. Yspaddaden lays numerous obligations upon Culhwch; he cannot marry Olwen without fulfilling them. One involves hunting the boar Twrch Trwyth, which cannot be achieved without the aid of Mabon son of Modron, who was "...taken from his mother when three nights old, and it is not known where he now is, nor whether he is living or dead."

In their quest for one who knows of Mabon's whereabouts, Arthur's men question a series of wise animals:

They went forward until they came to the Ousel of Cilgwri. And Gwrhyr adjured her for the sake of Heaven, saying, "Tell me if thou knowest aught of Mabon the son of Modron, who was taken when three nights old from between his mother and the wall." And the Ousel answered, "When I first came here, there was a smith's anvil in this place, and I was then a young bird; and from that time no work has been done upon it, save the pecking of my beak every evening, and now there is not so much as the size of a nut remaining thereof; yet the vengeance of Heaven be upon me, if during all that time I have ever heard of the man for whom you inquire. Nevertheless I will do that which is right, and that which it is fitting that I should do for an embassy from Arthur. There is a race of animals who were formed before me, and I will be your guide to them."

So they proceeded to the place where was the Stag of

Redynvre. "Stag of Redynvre, behold we are come to thee, an embassy from Arthur, for we have not heard of any animal older than thou. Say, knowest thou aught of Mabon the son of Modron, who was taken from his mother when three nights old?" The Stag said, "When first I came hither, there was a plain all around me, without any trees save one oak sapling, which grew up to be an oak with an hundred branches. And that oak has since perished, so that now nothing remains of it but the withered stump; and from that day to this I have been here, yet have I never heard of the man for whom you inquire. Nevertheless, being an embassy from Arthur, I will be your guide to the place where there is an animal which was formed before I was."

So they proceeded to the place where was the Owl of Cwm Cawlwyd. "Owl of Cwm Cawlwyd, here is an embassy from Arthur; knowest thou aught of Mabon the son of Modron, who was taken after three nights from his mother?" "If I knew I would tell you. When first I came hither, the wide valley you see was a wooded glen. And a race of men came and rooted it up. And there grew there a second wood; and this wood is the third. My wings, are they not withered stumps? Yet all this time, even until to-day, I have never heard of the man for whom you inquire. Nevertheless, I will be the guide of Arthur's embassy until you come to the place where is the oldest animal in this world, and the one that has travelled most, the Eagle of Gwern Abwy."

Gwrhyr said, "Eagle of Gwern Abwy, we have come to thee an embassy from Arthur, to ask thee if thou knowest aught of Mabon the son of Modron, who was taken from his mother when he was three nights old." The Eagle said, "I have been here for a great space of time, and when I first came hither there was a rock here, from the top of which I pecked at the stars every evening; and now it is not so much as a span high. From that day to this I have been here, and I have never heard of the man for whom you inquire, except once when I went in search of food as far as Llyn Llyw. And when I came there, I struck my talons into a salmon, thinking he would serve me as food for a long time. But he drew me into the deep, and I was scarcely able to escape from him. After that I went with my whole kindred to attack him, and to try to destroy him, but he sent messengers, and made peace with me; and came and besought me to take fifty fish spears out of his back. Unless he know something of him whom you seek, I cannot tell who may. However, I will guide you to the place where he is."

So they went thither; and the Eagle said, "Salmon of Llyn Llyw, I have come to thee with an embassy from Arthur, to ask thee if thou knowest aught concerning Mabon the son of Modron, who was taken away at three nights old from his mother." "As much as I know I will tell thee. With every tide I go along the river upwards, until I come near to the walls of Gloucester, and there have I found such wrong as I never found elsewhere; and to the end that ye may give credence thereto, let one of you go thither upon each of my two shoulders." So Kai and Gwrhyr Gwalstawt Ieithoedd went upon the two shoulders of the salmon, and they proceeded until they came unto the wall of the prison, and they heard a great wailing and lamenting from the dungeon. Said Gwrhyr, "Who is it that laments in this house of stone?" "Alas, there is reason enough for whoever is here to lament. It is Mabon the son of Modron who is here imprisoned; and no imprisonment was ever so grievous as mine, neither that of Lludd Llaw Ereint, nor that of Greid the son of Eri." "Hast thou hope of being released for gold or for silver, or for any gifts of wealth, or through battle and fighting?" "By fighting will whatever I may gain be obtained."

Then they went thence, and returned to Arthur, and they told him where Mabon the son of Modron was imprisoned. And Arthur summoned the warriors of the Island, and they *journeyed as far as Gloucester, to the place where Mabon was in prison. Kai and Bedwyr went upon the shoulders of the fish, whilst the warriors of Arthur attacked the castle. And Kai broke through the wall into the dungeon, and brought away the prisoner upon his back, whilst the fight was going on between the warriors. And Arthur returned home, and Mabon with him at liberty.*

(from *The Mabinogion*, Lady Charlotte Guest's translation).

An ousel is a blackbird; Cilgwri is the Welsh name for Wirral. So Arthur's men came to Wirral seeking wisdom from an elderly local blackbird!

Sir Gawain

The next Arthurian story to mention Wirral comes from a manuscript roughly contemporary with the *Red Book of Hergest.*

In *Sir Gawayne and the Grene Knight* Sir Gawain rashly accepts a challenge one New Year from a giant green knight who rides into Arthur's court. The Green Knight says that he will let anyone strike him with an axe on the condition that he can give a return blow in a year's time. Gawain decapitates the giant, but the headless body picks up its head, which tells Gawain to meet him at the Green Chapel in a year to fulfil the agreement.

Ten months later, Gawain rides north from Arthur's court. Eventually, Sir Gawain reaches the Castle Hautdesert where he stays for Christmas with its owner, Sir Bertilac. Here he learns of the Green Chapel's location, where he faces his final test.

A theory has been put forward that Sir John Stanley (see the chapter on Storeton) was the poet who composed the poem. Various clues suggest that the anonymous poet came from the vicinity of Wirral, and certainly he mentions the peninsula, though in less than flattering terms.

The poem itself is written in the medieval dialect spoken in Cheshire, and it is noticeable that the picture of Arthur's kingdom is vague until it reaches North Wales and Wirral. The story it tells is as follows:

One New Year's Eve when King Arthur and his knights were still young, they were feasting at Camelot when a strange, unearthly figure entered the hall. It was a huge man who rode on the back of a great horse and carried in one hand a massive axe and in the other a small holly tree, but the strangest thing about the man was that he was green. Not only were all his clothes green but so was his skin and even his hair.

He reined his horse in the middle of the hall, flung down the holly and cried out: "I would speak with the lord of this hall!"

All sat in silence, until Arthur spoke.

"I am lord of this hall. Come, sir, dismount and join our feasting."

"I will not," said the Green Knight. "I do not come here to feast, nor yet to fight. Yet word has come to me of the valour of your knights and I wish to put it to the test."

"I am sure you will find many of my men willing to joust with you," said Arthur.

"It is another test of valour that I have in mind," the Green Knight told him. "Let any man take from my hand this great axe and let him strike one blow with it in the place of my choosing. And first he must swear to give me the right to return the blow in the same place, if

I can, a year and a day from now."

Again silence filled the hall, and the knights exchanged glances and looked away again. None spoke, or took up the stranger's challenge.

The Green Knight laughed. "Is this King Arthur's hall at Camelot? Are you the Knights of the Round Table of whom I have heard? Hang your heads in shame: I see I have had a wasted journey!"

Arthur leapt up. "I will accept your challenge!" he cried.

But at the same time, Sir Gawain rose. "My lord king, permit me to claim this adventure."

Sir Gawain was Arthur's nephew, the son of his sister by Lot of Orkney, and one of the best knights of the Round Table. Graciously, Arthur acceded to his nephew's request.

Sir Gawain went to join the Green Knight, who boomed, "I am glad that I have found one worthy man in King Arthur's hall. What do they call you?"

"I am Gawain, son of Lot of Orkney, and nephew to the king. And whom do I address?"

"Men call me the Knight of the Green Chapel," the Green Knight replied. "Swear now to this bargain. You will strike one blow in the place of my choosing. And in a year and a day, you will accept my blow in return."

"By my knighthood I swear it," said Sir Gawain.

"Take the axe and ready yourself to do as I say."

Gawain took the axe. The Green Knight knelt down before him and bared his neck.

"Here you must strike," said the Knight.

Gawain lifted the great axe, then brought it hissing down. It cut straight through the skin, flesh and bone of the Green Knight's neck and the giant's head went rolling across the rush-strewn flagstones. Gawain waited for the trunk to collapse.

To his horror, and the horror of all present, the body rose and went after its head. Then it mounted the horse and held the head high, and the Green Knight's severed head spoke. "Keep your oath," he instructed Gawain, "and come to me in a year and a day."

And he rode from the hall.

The next winter, Sir Gawain rode out from Camelot on his horse Gringolet and went in search of the Green Knight, knowing as he did so that the quest could only end in his own death at the hands of the uncanny stranger. He rode aimlessly through the mountains of North Wales, where he had encounters with serpents and wolves, woodwoses and ogres, and had to sleep in the sleet and the drizzle amongst the rocks. Yet wherever he went, no one could tell him where lived a Green Knight, nor where lay the Green Chapel.

Passing Anglesey on his left hand he came down to ford the Dee by St. Winifred's Well, and rode on into the Forest of Wirral, where dwelt few who loved God or man. It was Christmas Eve when he followed an old paved road out of the trees and saw before him a snow-covered meadow and a fair stream, and beyond it a great stone hall. Thanking God for his mercy, Sir Gawain rode up to the gate and beat upon it with his sword pommel.

The door opened and a porter appeared.

"Good fellow," said Sir Gawain, "tell your master that a knight of Arthur's court is without and that he seeks shelter for himself and his horse."

The porter welcomed the knight and took him into the courtyard where squires hurried forward to take his steed before he was led into the Hall. Here the lord of the place stood before a roaring fire; a big, bearded man with flaming red hair. He gave Sir Gawain a fulsome welcome, and introduced himself as Sir Bertilac de Hautdesert.

"Thanks, noble sir," Sir Gawain replied. "God be good to you."

The squires led Gawain to the guest chamber and helped him disarm. Then they brought him a robe of ermine and took him back to the hall to eat with Sir Bertilac.

When supper was over, Sir Bertilac led Sir Gawain into another chamber to meet his lady. She sat by the fire with a lapdog on her knee and her maidens accompanying her, and with them an elderly lady. Sir Gawain thought her the fairest lady he had seen, though the old woman who accompanied the others was less to his taste. He spent four days with Sir Bertilac and his lady, and the hall was filled with Christmas cheer and rejoicing. On the fourth day, however, Sir Gawain told his hosts that he must continue with his quest. They both urged him to remain.

"I have stayed too long," he said. "I must meet the Knight of the Green Chapel at noon on New Year's Day, and yet I do not know where the Green Chapel is!"

Sir Bertilac laughed. "Then you are in the best place!" he said. "The Green Chapel is but two hours ride from here. Remain with us until New Year, and then one of my squires will take you there in time for noon!"

"Then I will stay here gladly," Sir Gawain replied. "Now it seems that I have achieved my quest."

"We have three days, then," said Sir Bertilac. "I shall spend them as I always do, hunting in the forest. But you must remain here and take your ease, and keep my wife company. In the evenings we shall all make merry."

Gawain agreed to this. Sir Bertilac laughed, and

added, "Christmas is a time for games. Let us make a solemn compact. I shall give you whatever I gain during my day's hunting, while you too give me whatever you receive while you remain in my hall."

"Gladly will I swear to this," Gawain replied.

The next day Sir Bertilac set out with all his squires and companions to hunt in the Forest, while, Gawain lay in bed. Soon the lady came to him and sat on the edge of the bed. Gawain became aware of her presence but pretended he was still asleep. She was aware of this and she began to tease him. They spent some time talking and she flirted with him, and he spoke courteously in return. When the lady rose to leave, she said:

"It has been pleasant, yet I cannot believe that you are the Sir Gawain they speak of."

"Why is that?" Sir Gawain was startled.

"Would Sir Gawain spend so long with a lady and yet never ask for a kiss?"

A little unwillingly Sir Gawain asked his host's wife for a kiss and she did so before going on her way.

That evening, Sir Bertilac returned from his hunting in the Forest with a red deer slung over the back of a pony. He told his huntsman to present it to Sir Gawain.

"In accordance with our compact," he said, "here are my spoils of the day."

"I thank you, sir," Gawain replied. "And I shall give in return what I gained today." And he gave the man a kiss.

Sir Bertilac laughed, and thanked him wryly. "And how did you come by that?" he asked.

"No," said Gawain, "that was not in our agreement." And Sir Bertilac left it at that.

Next morning Sir Bertilac went hunting again, while Sir Gawain again lay drowsily in bed. Soon the lady came to join him again, and again she flirted with him, trying to coax flirtatious words from her guest too. Sir Gawain was unfailingly courteous but turned her words aside as lightly as he could. And yet this time she gave him two kisses before leaving.

In the evening, Sir Bertilac returned home with the carcase of a bear which his huntsmen laid at Gawain's feet. Gawain thanked him for the spoils of the hunt, and in return gave him two kisses, his own spoils.

The next morning, while Sir Bertilac went hunting, Sir Gawain woke from uneasy dreams to find the lady bending over him. Again she flirted and begged him for kisses, but although she won three from him, he was more solemn than before because he knew that the next day he would go to his encounter with the Green Knight at the Green Chapel.

"Give me something to remember you by," she said wistfully.

"I have nothing to give," he said sadly.

"Then let me give you something of mine," she said, and offered him a green girdle.

"Lady, I cannot be your knight nor wear your favour."

She told him that he need not wear it openly, and that magic was woven into it, that the wearer would have a charmed life. Hearing this, Gawain was tempted, and he took the girdle and concealed it beneath his shirt.

That evening Sir Bertilac returned with nothing but a fox, which he gave to Sir Gawain with his apologies. In return, Sir Gawain gave him the three kisses he had received from Bertilac's wife. But he retained the green girdle.

The next day was New Year's Day, and Sir Gawain rose early, having slept very little that night. He made sure the green girdle was beneath his shirt and called to the squires to arm him. When he was armed, he went down to the courtyard where the squires brought out his horse Gringolet.

Accompanied by a single squire to show him the way, Sir Gawain rode out across the meadow and into the forest. Two hours' journey through wood and heath took him to the top of a valley where a little waterfall tumbled into a ravine.

"Sir," said the squire, "down there you will find the Green Chapel where the Green Knight awaits you. But do not go, sir, for he will slay you as he slays everyone he fights."

Gawain thanked him. "But my honour would be lost if I were to turn back now."

The squire directed him to follow the path along the side of the valley, which would take him to the banks of a stream, and the Green Chapel lay beside it. Dolefully, the squire left Gawain, clearly expecting never to see him again.

Gawain followed the directions and came down into the valley, but he could see no chapel by the stream, only a low green mound from which he heard the ominous sound of a blade being sharpened on a whetstone. He dismounted when he reached it, hitched Gringolet's bridle to an alder branch, then called, "Knight of the Green Chapel, I come as I swore I would."

The sound of the whetstone ended and a figure appeared from the mound, a tall man dressed in green, with green face and green beard. In his hand was an axe and Gawain knew that it was this he had heard being whetted.

"Welcome, Sir Gawain!" said the Green Knight.

"Now remove your helm and kneel before me. I must repay the stroke you dealt me in Camelot a year and a day before."

Gawain did as the Green Knight said. He removed his helm, thrust back his coif, knelt down in the mud and lowered his head. But when the Green Knight lifted the axe then brought it swishing down, Sir Gawain flinched away and the axe missed.

The Green Knight taunted him for his faint heart. "When it was you swinging the axe," he said, "I did not flinch."

"Yet I do not know that when my head is off I will be able to put it back on my shoulders as you did," said Gawain. He knelt again. "I will not shrink this time."

Again the Green Knight lifted his axe and again he brought it whizzing down, but again it missed and thudded into the earth, though Sir Gawain had not moved.

Gawain was angry. "Strike!" he cried. "Do not play with me!"

A third time, and Gawain knelt once more and the Green Knight brought the axe down and this time the sharp edge brushed the skin of Gawain's neck, but did no more. Eagerly Gawain leapt up.

"I have taken your blow and you have drawn blood," he said, "and now I am free of my vow and should you strike again, I may defend myself!"

Then he looked closely at the Green Knight, and he saw that although the man wore green, he was Sir Bertilac de Hautdesert, his host these last few days.

"You have indeed borne my blow," the Green Knight—Sir Bertilac—said. "I shall not strike again."

"Why then this game of three blows?" Gawain demanded.

"The first two that missed you, these were for the promise you kept truly, for the kiss my wife gave you when I rode hunting the first day, and the two the next day. The third blow that drew blood was for the promise that you broke when you gave me the three kisses but kept back the girdle. I know all that passed between you and my lady, for it was at my asking that she tempted you. As for the green girdle, you took it to save your life and I do not grudge you that."

Gawain produced the girdle and offered it him. "I am ashamed nonetheless," he said.

The Green Knight laughed, and said that few knights of the Round Table were more worthy than he, and asked him to return to his hall and spend the rest of the holiday in revelry. He revealed that the old lady Gawain had seen was none other than Morgan le Fay, the enchantress, who had devised the whole adventure to test the knights of the Round Table. Gawain had proved that their reputation was not ill-deserved. But Gawain would not return with him, but wished instead to ride back to Camelot and Arthur's court.

And so they parted.

King Horn

The last medieval poem to describe Wirral never refers to it by name. However, scholars such as WH Schofield (in The Story of Horn and Rimenhild) are sure that Westernesse, main location of the poem King Horn, is Wirral—its translation being 'peninsula in the west.' The name may be familiar to readers of Tolkien; he borrowed it from the medieval poem. The story is as follows:

1.

Long ago, when that land was called Suddene, there ruled over the Isle of Man a king named Murry, who had a wife called Godhild. She was the sweetest and gentlest of ladies, just as the king was the most virtuous of men. Despite this, they had only one child, a son named Horn, who spent the first twelve years of his life surrounded by loyal servants and devoted companions. Twelve friends went with him everywhere, joining him in sports and games and chivalrous exercises. Horn's favourite among these youths was Athulf, his most devoted companion, but next to him his closest friend was Fikenhild, who hid envy and hate beneath a show of love. Yet neither Horn nor Athulf suspected Fikenhild's falseness.

King Murry was riding along the cliffs of his island realm one day, accompanied by only two men, when something attracted his attention in a nearby bay. He galloped down to the shore where fifteen great ships were moored, packed to the bows with heathen pirates. Despite the huge numbers of hostile-looking men, the king rode up to them, followed by his companions, and asked, "What brings strangers into my land? What do you seek?"

The leader of the pirates, a man of great stature, said, "We come here to drive out the Christian law and bring this land back to heathen ways. We shall slay all those who put their faith in Christ. You shall we slay first."

The heathens attacked the three men and although King Murry and his companions fought valiantly, they soon fell to the heathens.

Without the king, the realm was defenceless, and the heathens spread throughout the land, burning and plundering, slaying all who would not renounce their Christian faith.

When the queen heard of her husband's death and saw the land burnt and plundered, she fled from the palace and abandoned all her friends and her son. Concealing herself in a solitary cave, she lived alone, continuing to worship Christ while the heathen seized control of the land. She prayed that God would protect her son Horn and that he would at last succeed his father as king.

But the heathens had captured Horn and his twelve friends and took the boys before the heathen leader. He was about to have them flayed alive when he saw the great beauty of Horn.

He asked him his name and on learning it he said, "Horn, you are a bold and valiant lad, tall for your age and strong, though I know you have not yet reached your full strength. Were I to release you and your friends I would regret it, for you will become great champions of your faith and will slay many of my people. You must die. But because you are all such noble lads, I will not have your blood on my hands; rather I will have you set adrift in a rudderless ship and consigned to the mercy of the waves, where Fate may have it that you will all be drowned.'

The boys wept and wailed as the heathens took them to the shore and placed them aboard the boat. As the current took them out to sea, Horn, who was the only lad not lamenting their fate, found a pair of oars and began to row in the same direction. Soon they were out of sight of the shore. Despite the despair of his companions, Horn rowed all night and only rested on his oars for weariness when dawn came over the sea.

As the light grew, Horn stood up and looked eastwards. He gave a great cry of joy.

"Friends!" he said. "I see land not far away. Listen, and you will hear the cries of the birds. Look, and see the green grass of this new country. Our lives are saved."

Athulf rose and saw what Horn had seen, the coastline of another land on the horizon. He began to cheer the others while Horn guided the boat to safe landing on the wide sands of Westernesse, as Wirral was named in those days. The boys leapt onto the shore, none but Horn giving any thought to their voyage, but Horn looked sadly at the boat that had guided them out of such trials. He pushed it back out to sea, then he and his friends turned and made their way towards the town they saw in the distance.

As they made their way wearily towards the town, they saw a man riding towards them. When he came nearer they could see that he was a man of high rank. Indeed it was, for this was Aylmer, who at that time ruled over Westernesse.

"Where do you come from, boys? Never did I see such strong, handsome youths in the land of Westernesse. Tell me where you come from and what you seek here."

Horn answered. "We are lads of noble birth from Suddene, which has been seized by heathens who have slain our fathers. They pitied us for our youth, and set us adrift upon the sea. After a night's voyage we found ourselves on the shores of this land. Now we are in your power and you may do what you will, but I pray that you will take pity on us."

King Aylmer was touched by his words, and he said, "You shall know only my help. But tell me your name."

Horn told him. Aylmer replied, "Horn! That is a good name. May this horn ring out across many lands. Come with me and be my son."

The king rode back to his hall and the youths followed on foot, but Aylmer found a horse for Horn, who rode at his side. When they entered the king's hall, Aylmer summoned his steward, a noble old man named Athelbrus, and put the boys in his charge, instructing him to train them as pages and squires, and to teach Horn particularly in woodcraft and fishing, hunting and hawking, harping and singing, and how to carve meat and serve mead at feasts, training him to be a knight. Athelbrus obeyed and took the boys on. Soon they found themselves learning the duties of life at court, which they took to with skill, Horn in particular.

He became popular with the people of Westernesse, and was loved most of all by Rymenhild, daughter of the king. She fell so in love with him that she came close to losing her mind. She could not bring herself to speak to him and she fell into sorrow. She sent for Athelbrus and told him to take a message to Horn, saying that she lay ill in her chamber and asking him to come quickly. Athelbrus was unhappy with this. He thought that what she was thinking about the youth was very strange and so was her request that Horn be brought to her chamber.

He went to Horn's companion, Athulf.

"Athulf," he said, "disguise yourself as Horn, come with me to the bedchamber and speak privately to Rymenhild. I am afraid that she wishes to do him ill."

Athulf agreed and let Athelbrus lead him to the chamber. Rymenhild, thinking he was Horn, sat him on her bed and put her arms around him.

"Horn," she told him, "I have loved you passionately for a long time. Plight your troth to me here and take me to wife. You will be my husband."

Athulf whispered in her ear, "You must say no more. I am not Horn, nor am I his equal. Even if he was under the earth or a thousand miles away, I would not deceive him or you."

Rymenhild blenched on learning who he was. She turned on Athelbrus. "Get you gone, you villain! You have lost all my favour. Leave my room and may ill luck accompany you! May shame seize you and hang you high on the gallows! It was not Horn I spoke with. Horn is more handsome by far. You must die a shameful death for this!"

Athelbrus fell to his knees. "My lady, listen! I hesitated to bring Horn to you because he is so fair and handsome. Aylmer placed him in my care. If Horn were here I would suspect that you would take pleasure of each other, and that would make the king sorry. Forgive my anger and I shall fetch Horn to you no matter who knows."

Rymenhild said, "Go at once and send him here after noon. When the king goes to hunt in the woods, no one will betray him. Horn shall stay with me until evening and I will have my way with him. I do not care what people will say to me afterwards."

Athelbrus went away. He found Horn in the hall,

pouring wine for the king.

"Horn," he said, "After the meal you must go quietly to Rymenhild's chamber to tarry with her. You will not regret it if you do."

Horn listened to the steward and after the meal he went at once to Rymenhild. He said, "Well may you sit, and comfortably, Rymenhild the bright—with your six maidens who sit with you. Our king's steward sent me to your chamber to speak with you. Tell me what you want. I will listen."

Rymenhild rose. She took him by the hand and sat him on the fur coverlet, gave him wine to drink his fill, made him good cheer and rained kisses upon his face and lips.

"Horn," she said, "without argument you shall take me as your wife. Horn, pity me and plight your troth."

Horn thought for a while. "Christ guide you," he said at last, "and give you heaven's bliss with your husband whoever he may be. I am too lowborn to marry you. I am a foundling. It would be no fair wedding between us."

Then Rymenhild was angry. She sighed sorely, threw up her arms and fell in a swoon. Horn was filled with sorrow and he took her in his arms and began to kiss her. "Beloved, dear, you must control your heart. Help me to become a knight, use all your influence with the king so he dubs me knight, so my lowly status be changed to greatness, and I will be worthy of your love."

Rymenhild had awoken from her swoon. "Quickly, Horn, it shall be done. You shall be made a knight before the week is out. Take this cup and also this ring to Athelbrus the steward, and make sure that he keeps this agreement. Say that I beseech him with the most passionate words that he go before the king in his hall, humble himself, and ask the king at once to make you a knight. He will be rewarded with silver and gold."

Horn left, since it was nearly evening, and he sought out Athelbrus, gave him the tokens and told him how he had fared and what he needed, and promised Athelbrus his reward.

Athelbrus hurriedly went to the hall and addressed the king.

"King," he said, "tomorrow you will wear your crown and celebrate your festival. You would lose little by dubbing Horn as a knight, to bear arms for you. He would be a good knight."

The king replied, "That would be well done. Horn pleases me. He will be a good knight. I shall dub him and afterwards he shall become my favourite, and he shall make his companions knights as well before me this very night."

Aylmer sat in thought long until the sun rose. Horn came before the king with his twelve companions. Aylmer dubbed Horn a knight with bright sword and spurs, placed him on a white horse, struck him a gentle blow and told him to be a good knight.

Then Athulf fell on his knees before Aylmer, and said, "King so bold, grant me a boon! Now that Horn is a knight, he who was born in Suddene, he is lord of lands and lord over us, who stand with him. He bears your arms upon his shield. Let him knight us all, for such is our right."

Aylmer replied, "Do as you wish." Horn dismounted and dubbed all his companions knights.

The feast was merry, and with fair entertainment, but Rymenhild did not attend because it was a feast for knights alone, and it seemed like an age before it ended. When it was over she sent for Horn and he went to her chamber with Athulf accompanying him.

Rymenhild greeted them, and she reminded Horn of what they had agreed. "If you are true in deed," she added, "you will do as you said. Now that you are able, release me from my pain."

"Rymenhild, be silent," he said. "When the time is right I will do all you wish. I shall prove my knighthood before I begin to woo you. We are young knights, and it is our manner that we will fight for our lady-loves before we can marry. If Christ blesses me I shall do deeds of prowess for your love. If I return alive from the fight, I shall take you as wife."

"Knight," she said, "truly I think I believe you. Now take this gold ring, on which is engraved the words 'Rymenhild the Young,' and wear it for my love. The stones upon it have such virtue that you will never be afraid of blows or be crazed in battle if you look upon it with your lady love in mind. And Sir Athulf, your brother, shall have another. Horn, I beseech you with ardent words, Christ give you good success and bring you home again."

The knight kissed her and she blessed him. He took his leave of her and went into the hall. The knights went to table while Horn entered the stables where he took his coal-black horse. It shook its armour and the court resounded, and as it began to leap, Horn sang merrily.

Horn rode on for over a mile until he came to the sea where he found a ship riding at anchor, crewed by heathens. He asked them what they sought or what brought them to this land.

One of the heathens looked at him and said arrogantly, "This land we will burn and we will slay those who live here."

Horn gripped his sword and attacked the heathens,

hewing off heads. The heathens surrounded him but he looked at the ring and thought of Rymenhild.

He slew them all, and set the leader's head on his sword point. Then he rode back to the hall and addressed the king.

"King," he said, "Well might you sit and all your knights with you. Today, after my knighting, I rode out at my pleasure. I found a ship by the shore crewed with the heathen. They attacked me but my sword did not fail me and I cut them all down or gave them severe wounds. I have brought you the head of their leader. Now are you repaid for making me a knight."

2

The next morning, the king went out hunting. He left Fikenhild behind. Now Horn went to Rymenhild's chamber where he saw her sitting in the sun, weeping piteously.

Horn said, "Love, your mercy, why do you weep so sorely?"

She said, "I do not weep for nothing, but while I lay asleep I cast my net into the sea and it would not endure. A great fish burst my net and I knew that I would lose the fish I would choose to keep."

"Christ and Saint Stephen," said Horn, "change your dream! I shall neither deceive you nor do anything you do not want. I shall make myself your own to hold and to know above all other creatures and to this I pledge my word."

Rymenhild wept but Horn stilled her tears.

"Beloved," he said, "Dearest, you shall hear more. Your dream will turn or else some man shall harm us. The fish that breaks the line—truly he will pain us. That which shall cause us anguish shall soon be seen."

As Aylmer rode by the river, Horn lay in the bedchamber.

When he returned, the king was greeted by Fikenhild, who had seen Horn enter Rymenhild's chamber.

"Aylmer, I warn you," he said, consumed by envy, "Horn will kill you! I heard what he said, and he bared his sword to take your life and take Rymenhild to wife. He lies in her bedchamber under her bedcovers, as he often does. Go there at once and you will find him there—then send him out of these lands or else he will harm you!"

Angry and sorrowful, Aylmer went to the bedchamber. He found Horn and Rymenhild in bed.

"Out, away!" he said. "Foul thief, you will nevermore be loved by me! Go out of my bedchamber and ill fortune accompany you. Unless you flee at once I shall strike out with my sword. Leave my lands or else I will slay you!"

Horn saddled his steed and put on his armour, lacing his corselet as if riding to battle, grasping his sword, not staying too long. At once he went from Rymenhild his betrothed, saying:

"Dearest beloved! Now you have your dream! The fish that broke your net has sent me away from you. Rymenhild, have a good day. I may no longer stay with you. Into unknown lands will I further go, and there I shall stay for seven years. At the end of seven years, if I have not come or sent a message, take yourself a husband, wait no longer for me. Clasp me in your arms and kiss me well and long."

She kissed him then fell to the ground in a swoon.

Horn took his leave; he could no longer stay. He took

Athulf, his brother, around the neck and said, "Knight so true, keep well my new love. You have never forsaken me. Keep and guard Rymenhild."

He mounted his horse and rode forth, going to the harbour where he hired a ship that would take him to the western lands. Athulf's eyes were weeping as he saw all this.

3.

The sea breeze rose up and drove Horn to Ireland. He set himself on the land and placed his foot in the stirrup. By the wayside he found two kings' sons, Harold and Berild. Berild asked him his name, and what he wanted.

"I am called Cuthbert," Horn replied, "and I have come ashore to seek my fortune."

Berild rode near him and took him by the bridle. "I hope I find you well, knight. Come and stay with me for a space. Might I die if you don't serve King Thurston! I never saw in my life so fair a knight!"

He led "Cuthbert" into the hall and fell to one knee, made him kneel and greet the good King. Then Berild said, "Father, you should take him on. Set him to ward your land, and no man shall harm it, for he is the best man that ever yet came to your kingdom."

Then the king said, "You are welcome here! Go now, Berild, quickly, and make him happy. When you go a-wooing, entrust him with your glove, but if you intend to marry, he'll drive you away, because of Cuthbert's handsomeness, assuredly you'll never succeed."

At Christmas, there came in at noon a giant heathen, fully armed, and said, "Sit still, sire, and listen to these news. Here are heathens arrived, many more than five here are on the sand, king, upon your land, one of them will fight against three knights. If the three slay him, all this land is yours; if they are overcome by their foe, all this land shall be ours. Tomorrow will be the fighting, when the light of day springs."

Then King Thurston said, "Cuthbert shall be one of them, Berild shall be another, the third Harold, his brother, because they are the strongest and the best at arms. But what counsel shall we take? I think that we will all die."

Cuthbert sat at the table and said these words: "Sire, it is not right for three to fight against one, three Christian men to fight against one heathen dog. Without any comrades, alone with my sword I shall easily bring three to death."

4.

The next morning the king woke, deep in sorrow. Cuthbert rose from his own bed and arrayed himself with his arms. He put on his corselet, laced it well and tightly and went to the King as he was rising.

"King," he said, "come to the field in order to see how we shall fight. We will go together."

At prime he rode out and found a bold giant with his companions beside him to await their death. Cuthbert entered the fight. He struck many blows, and the knights fell in a swoon.

He ceased his blows, for they most were slain, and said, "Knights, rest now a while, if you wish."

One heathen said he had never known such hard blows from a knight except for King Murry, who was so strong. Horn recognised the heathen leader who had driven him from the land, and who slew his father. He trembled, and his blood boiled; he drew his sword and looked upon his ring, thinking of Rymenhild. Then he stabbed the heathen leader through the heart.

The heathens, who had been so bold before, ran from him. Horn and his company sped after them and slew them all before they reached their ships. They bought Horn's father's death dearly. Of all the king's knights not one was harmed, but he saw his two sons Harold and Berild die before him.

The king wept. Men laid the dead princes on a bier and buried them.

The king went into his hall with all his knights. "Horn," he said, "You must do as I advise. My heirs are both slain, and you are a knight of great skill, of great strength, tall and fair of body. You shall marry my daughter Reynild, and rule my kingdom."

"Sire," said Horn, "it would be wrong for me to accept your daughter who you offer me, in order to govern your realm. I shall serve you better, sire, before you die. Before seven years are over your sorrow will change. When it has gone, sire, give me my reward. When I desire your daughter, you shall not refuse me her."

5.

Horn remained there for seven years. He sent no messages to Rymenhild nor did he go to her. Rymenhild remained in Westernesse, deeply sorrowful. A king visited and he wanted to marry her, so he made an agreement with Aylmer. The wedding was set for date in the near future, and Rymenhild dared not hesitate. She composed a letter and Athulf wrote it. Then she sent her messengers to every land to seek Horn, wherever men might find him.

Horn heard nothing of this until one day he went hunting in the woods. He met a boy there.

Horn said, "Dear friend, what do you seek here?"

"If it is your will, knight, I can soon tell you. I seek one Horn of Westernesse, on behalf of a maiden named Rymenhild. King Mody of Reynes will marry her and bring her to his bed. I have walked far along the seashore and he is nowhere to be found. Alas the hour! Alas the time! Now Rymenhild shall be led astray."

Horn spoke, with bitter tears, "Boy, good luck befall you! Horn stands before you. Go back to her again and say that she should not feel sorrow for I shall be with her by Sunday at prime."

The boy was very happy and he returned to his ship, but sadly he was drowned on the voyage. The sea threw him, dead, under Rymenhild's chamber wall. She undid the bolt of the house where she lived to see if she could see anything of Horn. When she found him drowned, the boy who she had sent to find Horn and should have brought him, she wrung her hands.

Horn came to King Thurston and gave him this news. He told him that Rymenhild was his own love, of the good family he came from, and how he had slain in the field the man who had killed his father. He added, "Wise king, repay me my service! Help me win Rymenhild! Do not fail me! I shall ensure your daughter is married to a good family. She shall have as husband Athulf, my good comrade, a good knight among the best and the truest."

The king said quietly, "Horn, have now what you desire."

He sent writs throughout Ireland, asking for brave knights, and enough men came to Horn that he soon went to his ships. He set out on his way in a good galley and the wind began to blow quickly. The sea drove him right to Westernesse. He struck sail and cast anchor before day had dawned or any bells had rung.

The word had spread of Rymenhild's wedding. Horn let his ship ride and went ashore. He told his followers wait by a wood's side. Horn went alone, and soon he met a palmer whom he greeted.

"Palmer, tell me your story."

The palmer said, "I was at the wedding of a maiden named Rymenhild. She could not stop herself from weeping. She said that she would not be married for gold, that she had a husband even if he were in another land. I was there at the gate. They let me in late. King Mody, the groom, ordered men to lead Rymenhild to her bedchamber. I stole away. I could not bear to see that sorrow. The bride weeps sorely, and it is great pity!"

Horn said, "Let us change clothes. You shall have my clothes, but give me your robe. I shall drink in the hall today, and some shall regret it."

The palmer laid down his robe and put on Horn's clothes, which were not unpleasing to him.

Horn took staff and wallet, fouled his face and dirtied his neck, making himself unbecoming, as he had never been before. He came to the gatewarden who spoke to him roughly. Horn asked him gently to open the door many times, but he might not succeed in coming inside. Horn turned to the gate and kicked the wicket. The rogue paid for his insolence: Horn threw him over the bridge so that his ribs cracked and then he went in through the gate.

He sat down in a low position in a row of beggars and looked about him. He saw Rymenhild sitting at the high table, looking as if she were out of her mind, weeping sorely and deeply, nor might any man stop her. He looked in every corner but nowhere did he see his comrade Athulf.

Meanwhile, Athulf was in the tower, looking out for Horn's arrival, if a ship would bring him. He saw the sea flowing, but no sign of Horn. This was his song:

"Horn, now thou art gone long.
Rymenhild thou me took
That I should look
I have a-kept her ever;
Come you now or never:
I may not longer her keep.
For sorrow now I weep."

Rymenhild rose from the table in order to pour wine, after meat in the hall, both wine and ale. She carried a horn in her hand, as the custom was in that land. Knights and squires all drank of the beer, but Horn alone had no share of it. Horn sat upon the ground, his thoughts bound up. He said, "Gracious queen, turn towards me, give to us among the first, the beggars are athirst."

She laid down her horn, and filled his cup a gallon

195

full from a brown bowl, for she thought he was a glutton.

She said, "Have this cup and this other thing with it. I believe I never saw a beggar so bold."

Horn gave it to his companion and said, "Dear queen, wine is not my desire unless it come from a horn. You think I am a beggar, but I am a fisherman come far east to fish at your feast. My net lies here, at hand on a fair shore. It has lain there fully seven years. I have come to see if it has taken any fish. I will drink nothing from any cup—I will drink to Horn from a horn. I have travelled from far away."

Rymenhild looked at him and her heart began to chill. She knew nothing of his fishing nor anything of Horn himself. She wondered why he told her to drink to Horn. She filled her horn with wine and drank to the pilgrim.

She said, "Drink your fill and then tell me truthfully if ever you saw Horn in the woods."

Horn drank from the horn and threw her ring into the bottom. He said, "Queen, now see what is in your drink."

The Queen went to her bedchamber with her four maidens. There she looked into the horn and found what he wanted, a gold ring which she had given to Horn. She feared that Horn were dead. She sent a maiden after the palmer.

"Truly, Palmer," she said, "The ring that you threw in the horn, tell me where you got it from and why you have come here."

He replied, "By Saint Giles, I have travelled many miles far beyond the west to seek my fortune. I found Horn about to go aboard ship. He said he would try to sail to Westernesse. The ship took to the tide with me and Horn the good. But Horn was ill, and he died during the voyage. He prayed fairly to me, 'Go with the ring to Rymenhild the young.' He has often kissed it — God rest his soul!"

Rymenhild said at once, "Heart, now you can burst, for Horn has you no longer, for whom you have pined so sorely."

She fell on her bed where she had hid her knife, to slay the loathed king and herself as well that same night if Horn did not come.

She set knife to heart and Horn quickly caught her. He wiped the dirt from his throat and said, "Queen so sweet and dear, I am your own Horn. Do you not know me? I am Horn of Westernesse. Kiss me in your arms!"

They kissed each other truly and were blissful.

"Rymenhild," he said, "I will go down to the end of the wood, where my knights are ready to fight, armed beneath their clothes. They shall anger the King and his guests who come to the feast. Today I shall teach them and strike them sorely."

Horn sprang out of the hall and let his cloak fall. The queen went to the chamber and found Athulf in the tower.

"Athulf," she said, "be happy and go swiftly to Horn. He is under the boughs of the wood and with him are many knights."

Athulf leapt with joy because of the news. He rode after Horn as quickly as his horse would go, overtook him indeed and was very happy. Horn took his company and showed them the way. He came in quickly (the gates were unlocked), heavily armed from foot to neck. Those who were inside except his twelve friends and King Aylmer, he made them all sorry they were at the feast. They left their lives there.

Horn did no vengeance on Fikenhild's false tongue. He made the others swear that they would never betray Horn even if he lay near death. He rang the bell for the wedding. Horn went with his men to the king's palace. There was a bridal feast for rich men to eat there. No tongue can tell the joy that was sung there.

Horn sat enthroned and bade them all listen.

"King," he said, "you shall listen to a tale among the best. I do not tell it to blame you: my name is Horn. You raised me to knighthood and I have proved my knighthood. Men told you, king, that I betrayed you and you made me a fugitive and I had to leave your land. You thought that I acted as if I had no thought but to lie with Rymenhild, and that I deny. But I shall undertake it until I win Suddene. Keep her for a time while I gain my heritage and to my realm. The land I shall obtain and I shall gain vengeance for my father. I shall be king of the town and wear the king's crown. Then Rymenhild shall lie with me."

Horn went to the ship with his Irish fellows—Athulf with him, his brother, he wanted no other.

6.

The ship began to make its way, the wind blew loudly. Within five days the ship arrived, at about midnight, on the coast of Suddene. Horn went ashore immediately; he took Athulf by the hand and went up to the shore. He found a knight lying asleep beside the road. Painted on his shield was a cross. Horn took hold of him and said, "Awaken, knight! Say what you are guarding and why you sleep here. I think, by your shining cross, that you belong to Our Lord. But you will show me this or I shall cut you to pieces."

The good knight rose in fear at the words.

He said, "Against my will I serve evil heathens. I was Christian once. Then there came to this isle heathens who made me forsake Christ, who I would have believed in. Against him they made me guard to keep this road against Horn, who is of age, and lives in the west, the best among knights. With their own hands they slew the king of this land and with him fell many hundreds, so it is strange that he does not come to fight. God grant him the right and the wind drive him here to end their lives. They slew King Murry, Horn's father, the courteous king. Then they sent Horn out of the land. Twelve comrades went with him, among them Athulf the good, my own child, my beloved son. If Horn is whole and sound and Athulf is without wound—he loves him so dearly and is so much a guide to him—if I could see the two of them, I would die of joy."

"Then be happy, knight, at this time most of all. Horn and Athulf his brother are both here."

The knight went to Horn and greeted him. He showed great joy while they were together.

"Children," he said, "how have you fared? Many

years have passed since I saw you. Will you win back this land and kill those who are in it?" He added, "Dear Horn, your mother Godhild still lives. She might have joy if she knew you still alive."

Horn said his speech: "Blessed be the time in which I come to Suddene with my Irishmen. We shall teach the dogs to speak our speech. We shall slay them all and quickly flay them."

Horn blew his horn and his people recognised it. They came out from the stern from under Horn's banner. He slew and fought all night and early morning and he left none of the kind heathens in the end.

Horn restored chapels and churches; he had bells rung and masses sung. Then he came to his mother's home in a wall of rock. He had a merry feast prepared. Joyous life he caused, but Rymenhild bought it dearly.

7.

Fikenhild was proud at heart and that pained him. He gave lavishly to young and old so they would be loyal to him. He had stone brought and hoped to succeed with it. He had a strong castle built and encircled with sea, where no-one could alight except the birds that flew. But when the tides withdrew, men could then come.

Fikenhild thought to harm Rymenhild. He began to woo her strongly, and the king did not dare refuse him. Rymenhild was full of anger. She wept tears of blood.

That night Horn sweated and dreamed heavily that Rymenhild, his mate, was brought into the ship. The ship began to lurch. His beloved would drown. Rymenhild undertook to swim to the shore. Fikenhild pushed against her with his sword's hilt.

Horn awoke out of sleep like a man in a hurry.

"Athulf," he said. "Comrade, we must go to ship. Fikenhild has done me wrong and caused Rymenhild distress. Christ, for his five wounds, drive me there tonight!"

Horn rode to the ship, his companions beside him.

Before the day dawned Fikenhild went at once to the King, asking for Rymenhild the bright, to wed her in the evening. He took her by night into his new fortress and he began the feast before the sun rose. Horn knew it before then; before the sun rose, his ship lay under the tower of Rymenhild's bedchamber. Rymenhild little knew that Horn was still alive. They did not know the castle because it was so new.

Horn found Arnoldin, who was Athulf's cousin, who was there at that time to wait for Horn.

"Horn," Arnoldin said, "king's son, well have you come to land. Today Fikenhild has married your sweet beloved, Rymenhild. I shall not lie to you: he has deceived you twice. He had made this tower for your sake. You may not go into it; no man may without contrivance. Horn, may Christ guide you so you do not lose Rymenhild."

Horn knew all the cunning that any man could know. He brought out a harp and took a few companions, skilful knights who disguised themselves as they pleased. He went along the beach towards the castle, sang merrily and made his harping heard.

Rymenhild heard it and asked what it was. Her attendants said they were harpers and some were fiddlers. They allowed Horn in at the gate of the hall and he sat down on a bench in order to hold his harp. He sang Rymenhild a lament. Rymenhild swooned and there were none who laughed. This went to Horn's heart so bitterly that it pained him. He looked at the ring and thought of Rymenhild. Then he went up to the table with a good sword. Fikenhild's head tumbled down, and Horn threw down all his men in a row.

When they were slain, he tore apart Fikenhild. For his meekness Horn made Arnoldin there king of all Westernesse after King Aylmer. The king and his vassals gave Arnoldin tribute. Horn took Rymenhild by the hand and led her to the shore, and he took with him Athelbrus, the good steward of his house. The tide rose and Horn set sail.

They arrived where King Mody was lord. Horn made Athelbrus their king for his good teaching. He showed all knights favour because of his knowledge of Horn's knights. Horn set sail and the wind blew him far. He arrived in Ireland where he found sadness; there he had Athulf wed the maid Reynild.

Horn came to Suddene, among all his kin. He made Rymenhild his queen, so all might be well.

Afterword

If Westernesse is to be identified as Wirral, as Schofield suggests, when exactly is the story set? The poem itself dates from the thirteenth century but it seems to refer to earlier times. The Saracens are clearly an anachronism; no Islamic corsairs were to be found in these waters before the Barbary Pirates, centuries later. However, pagan pirates of another denomination were a significant feature in the ninth to eleventh centuries; it is generally believed that the Saracens of King Horn were originally Vikings. The Norsemen settled in Wirral, as is well known, and many place names of Norse origin prove this. But is there evidence of an attack like the one in King Horn?

In the year 980, according to the Anglo-Saxon Chronicle, the Vikings renewed their attacks on England, raiding not only Southampton and Kent, but also Cheshire. *The Life of St. Werburgh* states that the Vikings ravaged Wirral and describes them as 'subreguli'—under-kings. They seem to have been the Vikings known to the Welsh Annals as the Black Host. Led by Gudrod Haraldsson, king of the Hebrides, these raiders terrorised the lands around the Irish Sea throughout the 970s and 980s. Gudrod seems to have had connections with the Isle of Man and he may have fought a battle there in 987; furthermore, he was killed in Ireland in 989. Could he be the inspiration for the Saracen leader in King Horn? The Saracen who attacked Suddene (the Isle of Man) and Westernesse (Wirral), and died fighting in Ireland?

If so, could the story of King Horn have its basis in fact? Perhaps it sheds some light on life in Wirral during the tenth century. Although Wirral's Viking settlement in the early 900s is chronicled, history otherwise remains silent until the Norman Conquest. Maybe the events of King Horn fill some of that gap. As for the name Westernesse itself, it represents an Old Norse original, *Vestrnes*. Perhaps this was the Viking name for Wirral.

APPENDICES

Appendix 1: Leland and Camden on Wirral

The king's antiquary, John Leland, writing about 1536, states that:

Wyrale begynnith lesse then a quarter of a mile of the very cite self of Chester, and withyn a 2. bow shottes of the suburbe without the northe gate at a litle brooket caullid Flokars Broke that ther cummith ynto Dee Ryver, and ther is a dok wherat at spring tide a ship may ly, and this place is caullid Porte Poole.

Half a myle lower ys Blaken Hedde, as an armelet of the grounde pointing oute. At this is an olde manor place longging to the Erle of Oxforde, and theryn lyith sumtyme Syr Gul. Norres.

A mile be water lower hard on the shore is a litle village caullid Sauheho (Saughall).

Lesse then a mile lower is Crabho (Crabhall).

A myle lower is Shottewik Castelle on the very shore longging to the King: and therby ys a park.

Shottewike townelet is a 3. quarters of a myle lower.

And 2. mile lower is a rode in D(ee) caullid Salthouse, wher again it (on the) shore is a salt house cotage.

Then is Burton hedde, whereby is a village almost a mile lower than Salt (House).

ii. myles lower and more is Denwale Rode, and agayne it a farme place caullid Denwaulle Haul. It longith to Mr. Smithe, and more up into the land is Denwaulle (Denhall) village.

ii. miles and more lower is Neston Rode, and ynward a mile ynto the land is Neston village.

About a 3. miles lower is a place caullid the Redde Bank, and ther half a mile withyn the land is a village caullid Thrustington (Thurstaston).

A mile and more lower is Weste Kirkeby a village hard on the shore.

And half a mile lower is Hillebyri, (Hilbre Point) as the very point of Wyrale.

This Hillebyri at the floode is al environed with water as an isle, and than the trajectus is a quarter of a mile over and 4. fadome depe of water, and at ebbe a man may go over the sand. It is about a mile in cumpace, and the grounde is sandy and hath conies. There was a celle of monkes of Chestre, and a pilgrimage of our Lady of Hilbyri.

The barre caullid Chester Barre that is at (the) very mouth of the sandes spreade oute of Dee Ryver is an 8. or 10. mile west south west from Hilbyri.

It is by estimation a XVI. mile from the point of Hilbery to crosse strait over to the next shore in Lancastershire.

For Lyrpoole (Liverpool) lyith a X. miles into the lande from the mouthe of Mersey Water, and lytle lak of XX. from the very barre of Mersey that lyith in the mayne se.

From the poynt of Hylbyri to Lirpoole as it lyith withyn the lande a X. mile.

From Hilbyri to cumpace about the shore of Wyral on

Mersey side to Walesey (Wallasey) village on the very shore, wher men use much to salten hering taken at the se by the mouth of Mersey, is a seven or eight miles.

Thens a 2. myles to the fery house on Wyrale shore, and there is the trajectus proximus to Lyrpole a 3. miles over.

Aboute half a quarter of (a) mile upward hard on Wyral shore is Byrk(et) a late a priory of a XVI. monkes as a celle to Chester without any village by it.

Al the shore grounde of Wyral upon Be side ys highe banked, but not veri hilly grounde. And so ys the bank of Wyrale onto Birket on Mersey side.

The trajectus from Hillebyri directely overthwart bytwixt Flint and Basingwerke is at the ful se a VII. miles over.

While Camden, in his Britannia (1607) says:

From the Citie [of Chester] Northwestward there shooteth out a languet [tongue] of land, or promontorie of the maine-land, into the sea, enclosed on the one side with Dee mouth, on the other side with the river Mersey. Wee call it Wirall, the Welsh Britans for that it is an angle terme it Kill-gury. In old time it was all forest and not inhabited, as the dwellers report, but King Edward the Third disforested it. Yet now beset it is with townes on everie side, howbeit more beholden to the sea than to the soile. For the land beareth small plentie of corne, the water yeeldeth great store of fish. At the entrie into it on the South side standeth Shotwich, a castle of the Kings, upon the salt water. Upon the North standeth Hooten, a manour which in King Richard the Second his time came to the Stanleies, who fetch their pedigree from Alane Sylvestre, upon whom Ranulph the first of that name, Earle of Chester, conferred the Bailly-wick of the Forest of Wirall, by delivering unto him an home. Close unto this is Poole, from whence the Lords of the place that have a long time flourished tooke their name, and hard by it Stanlaw, as the monkes of that place interprete it, a Stony hill, where John Lacy Connestable of Chester founded a little monasterie, which afterwards by reason of inundations was translated to Whaley in Lancashire. In the utmost brinke of this Promontorie lieth a small, hungrie, barren and sandie Isle called Il-bre, which had sometime a little cell of monkes in it.

Appendix 2: Sir William Stanley's Garland
    Containing
    His Twenty-One Years TRAVELS through most Parts
of the World: and his safe Return to Latham Hall.

Sir William Stanley's Travels.

IN Lancashire there liv'd a Lord,
A worthy Lord and a Man of Fame,
Whose dwelling was at Latham Hall,
And the Earl of Derby call'd by Name.
Which brought their Father great delight,
He brought them up in Learning good,
Whereby there Wisdom to requite.
The eldest was call'd my good Lord Strange,
Lord Fardinando was his Name;
The youngest was call'd Sir William Stanley,
A noble valiant minded Man.
But as it happen'd on a Day,
Sir William fell upon his knee,
Desiring Leave of his Father dead,
Some Foreign Countries for to see;
O grant me Leave, Father, he said,
Some Foreign Countries for to See;
To learn the Speech of other Lands,
Whereby I may renowned be,
I'll grant thee Leave, Son Will, he said,
For three Years Space thou shall be free,
And Gold and Silver thou'st have enough,
For to maintain the gallantly.
But before thou go take here my Ring,
Take care to keep it secreatly?
And if thou lackest any thing,
Be sure thou send the fame to me.

Then Sir William took leave of Latham Hall,
And of all that in lovely Latham lay,
And then he prepared him for the Seas,
To travel in some strange Country.
But so soon as Sir William was got on Ship board,
He to himself did Secretly say,
I'll make a Vow to the living Lord,
That three seven Years I'll make away,
Before to England I'll return,
Or ever on English Ground will tread;
Twenty One Years shall be past and gone.
According to the I've vow made,
Then first Sir William travell'd to France,
To learn the French Tongue and to dance
He tarried there not past three Years,
But he learned their Language and all their Affairs
And then Sir William would travel to Spain,
There for to learn the Spanish Tongue,
He tarried there not past half a Year.
But he thought he'd been in Spain too long.
To Italy then Sir William would go,
To Rome and to High-Garmany,
To view the Countries all around,
And see what pleasures in them might be.
In Rome and in High-Garmany,
He stayed three Years before he went,
And then to Aegypt he took his way, to view that
Court was his intent,
But one year and a half Sir William staid,
And took his leave most courteously,
Of the King of Morocco and his Nobles all,
Then went to the King of Barbary,
When two full Years Sir William had been,
Into Russia he needs must go,

To visit the Emperor and his Queen.
One Doctor Dee he met with there,
Which Doctor was born at Manchester,
Who knew Sir William Stanley well,
Tho' he had not seen him for many a Year.
Pray what's the Cause, the Doctor said,
Brings you Sir William into this Country;
I came to travel, Sir William reply'd
And I pray the Doctor what brought thee,
I came to do a Cure the Doctor said,
Which was of the Emperor's Feet to be done,
And I have perform'd it effectually,
Which none could do but an Englishman.
Then he brought him before the Emperor,
Who Entertain'd him with princely Cheer,
And gave him Gold and Silver store,
Desiring his Company for seven Years.
But one three Years Sir William would stay,
Within the Emperor's Court so freely,
And then Sir William he would go,
To Bethlehem right speedily.
Likewise to fair Jerusalem,
Where our Blessed Saviour Christ did die,
He asked them if it was so
They answered and told him aye,
This is the Tree, the Jews then said,
Whereon the Carpenter's Son did die
That was my Saviour Sir William said,
For sure he dy'd for the Sins of me.
But one half Year Sir William would stay,
He kiss'd the cross with weeping Eyes;
And then he would into Turky go,
Where he endured more Misery.
For passing through Constantinople,

Wherein the Great Turk did lie;
Sir William then was taken prisoner,
And for his Religion condemn'd to die,
Before I'll forsake my living Lord,
My blessed Saviour and sweet Lamb;
Sweet Jesus Christ that dy'd for me,
I'll die the worst of Death that e'er did Man,
Farewell Father, farewell Mother,
And farewell all Friends at Latham Hall;
Little do they know I am a Prisoner,
Or how I'm subject unto Thrall.
A Lady walking under the prison Wall,
Hearing Sir William sore lament;
Unto the Great Turk she did go,
To beg his Life was her intent.
A Boom a Boon thou Emperor,
For thou'rt a Lord of great Command;
Grant me the Life an of Englishman,
Therefore against me do not stand.
For I will make him a Husband of mine,
Whereby Mahomet he may adore;
He'll carry me into his own Country,
And safely thither conduct me o'er.
Take thou thy Boon, thou gay Lady,
For thou art one of a tender Heart;
But let him yield to marry thee,
Or let him be hang'd e'er he depart.
The Lady's to the Prison gone,
Where that Sir William he did lie;
Be of good Cheer thou Englishman,
I think this Day I've set the free.
If thou wilt yield to marry me
And take me for to be thy Bride;
To take me into thy own Country,

And safely thither to be my Guide,
I cannot marry, Sir William laid,
To ne'er a Lady in this Country;
For if ever on English Ground I tread,
I have a Wife and Children three.
This excuse serv'd Sir William well,
So this Lady was sorry for what he did say;
And gave him five hundred Pounds in Gold,
To carry him into his own Country.
But one half Year Sir William would stay,
After from prison he was set free
And then he would to Greenland go,
Where he endur'd more Misery
For three Months there was nothing but dark,
And there Sir William was forc'd to want,
He fed on nothing but Roots,
And they to him grew wond'rous scant
His Shoes was frozen to his feet,
He scarcely knew where for to tread;
On his Hands and Knees he was forc'd to creep
Expecting each hour he should be dead.
But when Day-light it did appear,
Lord in his heart he was full fain?
Then he saw Ships coming from merry England
To fetch whales Oil they thither came.
One Captain Stanley Owner o'th Ship;
When he saw Sir William, unto him he came
He had known him in his own Country
A Man of Noble birth and Fame,
You're welcome from Travel the owner said;
But scarce one word Sir William did say,
Until that he had to him sworn
Nor on ship board would he come that Day,
That he should never Name at Latham Hall,

Nor to no Friend as he should see,
Nor never his name in question call,
When he came into his own Country.
For three Years space I have to stay,
According to the vow I've made,
And those three Years shall have an end,
Or on English Ground I'll never tread.
Then back they all came for Holland,
Being joyful of Each Company.
And the Captain he took his leave of him,
And bid him welcome to the Low Country;
With one John Howell he met there,
For three Years space to be his man
To get his living at other Men's backs,
When all his Money was spent and gone.
But when those three Years was at an End,
Lord in his heart he was full-fain;
Then he saw Ships coming from merry England,
And to Latham Hall he return'd again.
But standing bare at Latham gate,
Desiring to speak with the old Earl;
The porter thrust him back again,
Much like unto a dogged Churl.
Go stand thee back, thou Fellow bare,
Thou cannot speak with my Lord this Day
Now I'll betide thee Sir William said,
I was as as well born and bred as thee
But he got Lodging at old Holland's House,
Who entertain'd him with good Cheer;
And when they were at Supper set,
He called for a Bottle of his best beer,
Now by your Leave good man Holland,
We'll drink a Health to an Englishman
Whom I have seen in Countries strange,

And William Stanley is his name.
Do you know my young Lord said old Holland,
I pray you, Sir, tell unto me;
He is no Lord, Sir William said,
But him I've seen in a far Country.
He is a Lord, said old Holland,
He is a Lord of high Degree;
For why his eldest Brother's dead,
And Sir William's in a far Conntry.
Old Holland got up betime in the Morn;
Before it was well break of Day,
To speak with the Earl of Derby then,
As he rode Hunting that Day.
Good Morrow, my Lord, said old Holland,
Last Night a Guest at my House did lie;
And come out of Countries strange,
And brings Tiding of your Son William Stanley.
Bring him hither to me, said the old Earl,
Let me see that Guest right speedily,
If he can tell me Tiding of my Son Will,
Then well rewarded he shall be.
But when he came his Father before,
Sir William fell upon his Knee;
Craving blessing of his Father dear.
And Pardon for all his Discourtesy.
If thou be my Son, Will, said the old Earl,
As I do very well think thou may be;
I gave thee a Ring, when thou didst go,
Restore the fame to me again
He gave his Father then the Ring,
Whereby he knew him perfectly;
And shew'd him a Lion on his right Side,
Which is a mark the Lord sent me.
The King then hearing he was come,

Sent for him straight way up to Court;
And entertain'd him Royally,
With gallant Cheer and Princely Sport
The Earl of Derby made a Feast,
Which lasted for Months three,
And nobly entertain'd his Guests,
That came to see his Son William Stanley.
FINIS.

Appendix 3: Excerpt from *The Struggles and Adventures of Christopher Tadpole*

CHAPTER X.
THE "RING O' BELLS" AT BIDSTON.

The calm and soothing twilight of spring eventide was gliding slowly onward upon the earth as Hickory led the donkey, upon which Christopher was seated, along a rude bridle-way towards the last halt he intended to make on their journey.

They were travelling along a bold headland, on the ridge of which their path lay. Hitherto they had gone for some little distance over broken ground, encumbered with huge blocks of stone, and dug into deep quarries and pits that it required some little caution to avoid in the failing light; but now they had arrived at a beaten track, and all was smooth before them. It was not yet so dark that Christopher could not observe the extensive panorama around him, although the horizon was already veiled in shade. But his attention was principally attracted by a swarm of lights that he was looking down upon on his right, the like of which he had never before witnessed.

They rose, bright and twinkling, even in the last gleam of day, one above the other, until the most distant and the faintest appeared to mingle with the peeping stars that one by one were coming out in the blue air. Their reflection gleamed and quivered in a great water that flowed between them and the headland; and they spangled the banks in long array, until they got so hazy at the far-off points, that they only caught the eye at intervals. But they were not all stationary. Upon the shore, and on the water, they moved along, crossing and re-crossing one another, and mixing with the general mass, until all appeared to be endowed with bewildering motion.

"That's a larger mine than we've got," said Christopher, as he looked in wonderment at the illumination, his only idea of a number of lights being connected with the working of the miners.

"It isn't a mine," replied Hickory, "as you shall see to-morrow. That's a great town, and those are the lamps. It's Liverpool."

As far as Christopher's knowledge was concerned, it might have been Kamschatka. But the sight was so riveting that he could not take his eyes from it, scarcely even to notice the lighthouse under whose very walls they passed, with its array of signal masts that looked as if somebody was either preparing a great display of fireworks, or making ready to set sail and carry the entire hill, lighthouse, telegraph and all, out to sea, upon the first fair wind.

"That's a curious thing," said Hickory, as he pointed to the telegraph. 'I've heard there's people can read that gibbet. Just like a L. I never could, not to speak of. I've made out a F, and a L, and a £ without the middle; and sometimes they was upsy-down. And once I saw it trying uncommon hard to turn itself into a H, but it wan't much of a go, not to speak of."

Whilst he was talking, he led the donkey from the ridge, and they descended towards a small nest of houses, as the hill shut out the expanse of view and the cluster of lights that had fixed Christopher's attention. Hickory's spirits seemed to rise as he got lower: mercurial, indeed, in their property. He sang so many snatches of songs, running one into the other with such wilful carelessness, that the brave old oak was getting up stairs on the banks of Allan water, and prevailing upon somebody to drink to him only with their eyes as he struck the light guitar all the day in the Bay of Biscay and allowed the bumper's toast to go round; and no one could have decided which air was his especial favourite. Nor did he stop until he arrived at the entrance of the hamlet.

It was a little, quiet, grey village — so very grey, indeed, and venerable, and quaint, that no flaunting red brick had dared to shew itself and break the uniform tint of its gabled antiquity. The houses were grey, and the wall-fences were grey, and so was the church tower. So also was the pedestal of the sun-dial in the grave-yard, that mutely spoke its lesson on corroding time to all who cared to heed it. And the old grange, with its mullioned windows and ivy-covered gateway, was the greyest of all: there was scarcely any surmising as to when it had been a green damp level young house. None could have given the information but the church tower: and when that spoke, it was but of the newly past, the fleeting present, or the call to the future Heaven.

Hickory led his little companion by the church, and at last they stopped at a small hostel, with which he seemed to be well acquainted. There was yet light enough for the sign to attract Christopher's attention. It represented a party of industrious individuals, one of whom was as grey as the village, performing certain of those triple-bob complications with ropes and bells, the achievement of which we at times read of in the newspapers, with as clear a notion of what task has been surmounted as though the chief actors in it had squared the circle, boxed the compass backwards, composed a fugue, or tried to pull down our sublimest creed to a peppery squabble of ecclesiastical stonework and linen-drapery.

And on the other side was quite a different picture. There was the lighthouse they had passed; and all the firework poles, and a windmill; and two huntsmen going up-hill like mad; and one more, who was not going to be beaten at any price, coming in at the side; and the fox at the top; all very exciting to behold, but withal calculated to confuse the mind of the casual traveller, as to the exact simple sign to be made out from all this pictorial display. It did not, however, perplex Hickory.

"Whoa!" he cried, as he halted at the door. "Here's the Ring o' Bells at Bidston, and here we'll put up for to-night. And there's the old tree t'other side, not cut down yet; not a leaf on him though; looks as if he was growing with his roots uppards. Are you tired, Christy?"

"I'm very hungry," replied the little boy.

"Ah! hunger's the best sauce," observed Hickory, "that's what makes the boys so impudent. Look there— can you read what's over the door? There's just light enough."

"S — I — Simon Croft," said Christopher, staring at the board.

"No — no— the poetry," continued Hickory; "that's first rate, mind you. Listen now: 'Walk in my friends' — that's you and I, you know; anybody, as the saying is; all his friends — * and taste my beer and liquor; if your pockets be well stored you'll find it come the quicker.* Very good — now go on from 'quicker.' "

"'But for want of that,' read Christopher, "'has c — a — u — ' "

"Has caused both grief and sorrow,' continued Hickory. " Therefore you must pay to-day, I will trust to-morrow.' Beautiful! how I should like to sing it.' "

And he commenced putting the words to music of his own, when the landlord appeared at the door.

"Here we is, master," said Hickory, who appeared to know the house. "Just a singing your poetry. You has precious few bad debts, I should think, after that."

"Middlingish, as times go, Hickory," said the landlord. "And how do you find yourself?"

"Oh, I find myself in nothink except my clothes," replied the other, "but you needn't be afraid. We've done capital. 'Pay to-day, I will trust to-morrow,'" he continued, reading and singing. "Ah! that does good, depend upon it; frightens 'em, eh?"

The landlord smiled as he took Christopher from the donkey, and put him on the ground; and wished it always did.

"It does, 'pend upon it," continued Hickory'; "anything like reading does always. When we was at Stratford and Avon we saw a tombstone there of a gent — one of us perfessionals — who's buried there; thinks a good deal of him too they does. And he's put on his tombstone as he wouldn't hare his orts meddled with on no account. They've never done it neither; no, not all the body-snatchers or doctors in London, nor Guys, nor anywheres. Bide there now."

He hung the halter of the donkey over the rails; but there was not much fear of his running away; and then taking Christopher by the hand, led him into the house, in the common room of which several people had assembled.

"Service to everybody," said Hickory, as he made a low bow in return for the attention his appearance excited. "How d'ye do, mum?" he added to the landlady.

"Well, Mr. Hickory'," returned the hostess, "Are you

come back again?"

"Yes, mum: here we is; like rats and poors-rates, no getting rid of us, as the saying is."

"Have you done well this last trip, Mr. Hickory?" inquired the hostess.

"We can't disactly grumble, mum. When we got enough to drink, we drink it; and when we didn't, we went without. We've not had radar fair play though."

"No! Mr. Hickory?"

"No, mum. It's painful to think about, but poor Luddy's gitting past his work. He does look uncommon sad for a merriman. And the more he paints hisself, the sadder he looks — that's the worst of it. He tried to bring up his mouth into a laugh with wermillon, but it was no go; it dropped into a horseshoe sort of a shape directly."

"Ah!" said Mrs. Croft, with a slight sigh of interest.

"And his wind ain't of no account neither," continued Hickory, "for the Pandaeans. There's more of the drum than the pipes in all his music; and as I say, you can't give a good notion of a tune not on a drum alone."

"We must all get old, Mr. Hickory," said the landlady.

"Yes, mum, we must. It's a complaint that don't seem to trouble you much though."

The landlady looked so pleasant!

"But it troubles Luddy," continued Hickory. "I wish the government would buy a theaytre, as a sort of paddock for old clowns where they could be found with fire and candles, and have all their larks amongst themselves, and offer one another their tuppences for the goodwill of firework-makers' shops and such like, and steal whatever they pleased, without being obliged to jump through windows and down coffee-mills out of the way afterwards. And how have you been, mum — busy?"

"Pretty well, since summer began, as you may see," replied Mrs. Croft, pointing to some hams that hung from the rafters of the quaint, old low-roofed room.

It should be mentioned that the summer season is not so dependant upon the Almanac at Bidston, as upon Good Friday; on which day it commences, whatever the state of the weather-glass. And with it begins also the consumption of ham and eggs at the "Ring o' Bells" in mighty quantities; you would have bad luck through the year if you did not eat of both to something beyond repletion on that day, in the more or less Elizabethan parlour of the hostel. And the hams form a sort of zodiac round the room, by the state of which you may calculate upon the progress of the season. Comfortable they look, too, in their canvass bags; and pleasant are the visions of crisp cupped rashers, and rich yolks blushing through their milk-white jackets, that they conjure up.

During this conversation, Christopher had been inspecting the company, and was finally lost in admiration of the scroll-work chalked on the floor. But the mention of ham and eggs attracted him directly, and he looked from Hickory to the landlady with his large eyes, which told as plainly as eyes could speak, that he should have no objection to increase the consumption.

"Not your little boy, Mr. Hickory?" asked Mrs. Croft.

"Not as I knows on, mum," replied the traveller, "although there is something of a likeness to be sure.'

Two or three of the guests laughed aloud, as they compared the features of the fair-haired child with Hickory's full-blown, weather-beaten visage.

"Ah — you may laugh, gents," said Hickory,

winking; "but it's the growing up as does it, and always by contrarey. Pretty babies always grows up ugly, and ugly ones pretty. I was uncommon ugly when I was a baby: and look at me now."

Here Hickory made a great fall in his back, and spun round in a comical fashion, finishing in an attitude, to the great delight of the lookers on.

"Well, he is a pretty little fellow, to be sure," said Mrs. Croft.

"Thankee, mum; and the same to you and many on 'em," replied Hickory with a bow.

"No — not you," said the landlady smiling, "I mean the child. Come here, little man. What's your name?"

"Christopher Tadpole, please," answered the child.

A fellow, in a rough countryman's dress, had been smoking at the fire-place with his head half up the chimney — evidently from habit, as the grate was now filled with flowers — but as he heard the boy give his name, he turned quickly round and fixed his eyes on him so earnestly, that as soon as Christopher caught the glance, he was almost frightened.

"Do you know the Westland mine, young 'un?" he asked. "I think you do— eh?"

The little fellow looked first at Hickory and then at the man, evidently in some fear. But he did not answer; he only shuffled up to the landlady.

"You needn't hide your head," continued the man, rising. "Let's have a look at you."

And he took the child by the arms, and hoisted him on to the table.

"You couldn't tell a bit of salt if you saw it now, I'll be bound," said the man.

"Yes, I could," answered Christopher; "that's a bit." And he eagerly pulled all that remained of the chrystal from his pocket, and shewed it to the others.

"So it is," said the man, going back to his settle. "That'll do; it's alright."

"Well; that's a matter of opinion," observed Hickory, who had been looking on somewhat amazed during the dialogue; "it don't seem to me as if it was. What do you know about this boy?"

"Nothink," surlily returned the man. "What do you?"

"Not quite so much," said Hickory. And then he looked round pleasantly at the company, feeling it necessary to re-establish the confidence that these questions might have shaken; and not at all anxious that Christopher should in any way be reclaimed or acknowledged, from the attraction he proved in the travelling company. But his mind was soon relieved. The man knocked the ashes out of his pipe upon the hob, and then got up to leave, quieting, by sundry cuffs, the restless movements of some animals who were jostling in his pockets, from which the head of a rabbit occasionally thrust itself as he went out.

Hickory ordered some supper, as soon as he was gone; and then producing a pack of cards proceeded to delude the company with furious cunning performances, changing spades into diamonds, and making knaves turn up where they were never suspected to be, and pronouncing complicated words — not to say utterly incomprehensible — which literally set Christopher aghast, and made him handle every card as though he expected it to go off. But all this increased the admiration of Hickory to the highest pitch.

"Now, gents; encourage the performance if you please," said the artist when he arrived at a becoming point of the entertainment. "We're not above copper, but take silver whenever we can get it; so don't be afraid of offending us. Now, gents!"

He rattled a box as he spoke, in which two decoy bad half-crowns had long resided, and went round to the people, who were not backward in contributing humble sums.

"Thank you, Sir," said Hickory; "the times is bad and wittles dear. I've been bring for the last two months at Wolverhampton upon stewed curry-combs and tin-tack puddings, which ain't good for delicate stomachs."

"I should reckon not," said one of them with a laugh.

"Oh! bless you — that's nothing. I know a nailer as has brought up a small family upon screw-drivers and sand-paper. Digest any tiling, they can, in manufacturing towns. Now, gents!"

"Try them out of doors," said a spectator, pointing to the window. "Why should they see it for nothing?"

The moon had risen, and its light fell upon the old grey church, and streamed through the casement upon the fancifully ornamented stone floor of the inn. As Hickory looked towards the window, he saw two outline forms apparently gazing into the room; but the minute attention appeared to be directed to them, they retired.

"That's shirking," said Hickory; "never mind, I'll try it on."

He went out at the door, with the intent to ask them for their contribution; but it was only to see them passing down the lane quickly.

"Ah!" he said, as he returned, "they outsiders is never of much count, as I know at the fairs. The money-box frightens 'em all away like a gun does crows. Never mind; we can pay for what we has: and now for supper."

Christopher's eyes brightened at the sound. The

word was given, and the eggs and ham were soon hissing on the fire in the kitchen, and then they fell to with appetites that almost made the rest of the company believe in the stories of manufacturing hunger that Hickory had been propagating. The dish was excellent, and the ale was something beyond that. Christopher drank out of a glass almost as tall as himself, until he laughed, and talked, and finally went to sleep on the floor in the comer of the room. Hickory kept the company together for a long time, with his songs and performances, until they insisted upon a second collection being made: and one enthusiastic gentleman declared he should come and stay a fortnight with him. There had not been so much ale drawn at the Ring o' Bells that year: not even on ham-thirsty Good Friday. So Mr. Croft said, and he was a man worthy of credence.

But at last the party broke up, and Hickory and Christopher were lodged in a contiguous loft upon some fresh hay — a species of couch the exhibitor far preferred to the bed of domestic life.

And then the old grey village slumbered in the tranquil moonlight; not a sound breaking its stilly repose except the low calling of the sea, whose murmurs lulled it into yet deeper quietude. The cold beams hung upon the ivied gateway of the manor, and lighted up the silent chancel of the church, as they marked unwonted hours in shadow upon the dial at the porch, and threw the branches of the dead tree into spectral relief against the deep blue sky. They bathed the gables with their silver flood, and twinkled in the small window panes of the inn: and a few rays stole between the tiles and fell upon Christopher, as he lay curled up asleep in a species of nest he had made in a truss of hay, too tired to dream either of his past existence or his future destiny.

Appendix 4: from *Gayton Wake* by Richard Llwyd

Villains, yes — our annals prove,
That this was long your name.
Though Scandal's self, with all her eyes,
Could nothing find to blame.

The Muse now hails your happier days;
Delighted calls you friends;
And pleas'd, from Arvon's, cliff her views.
To you and Gayton bends.

She loves, the joys, of rural life.
The paths by peasants trod,
Partakes unseen their harmless mirth,
And sings of MARY DOD.

Up rose the sun — the sky was clear,-
And gently ebb'd the Dee :
The winds of Heaven were fast asleep,
Though Gayton all was glee.

The lads of Wirral came in crowds,..
The nymphets, neat and trim;
To stay at home on such a day
Is very near a sin.

And Love, who never miss'd a wake,
Brought quivers fill'd with darts;
He's much to do on all such days,
And wound a world of hearts

And Cambria's youth from Edwin's shores-
An annual voyage take;

What lass would stay on that side Dee,
When Love's at Gayton Wake.

Nor ye despise a country wake,
Who crowd the fetes at Frogmore,
Who wheel from Brighton up to town,
And then wheel down to Bognor.

It much behoves you mighty folk,
Would hurry deign you leisure.
To think that life, your constant wake,
Be pass'd in harmless pleasure.

Youth, manhood, age, even childhood came;
To share this jocund day;
The hedges shone with gaudy shops.
And Gayton all was gay.

Dwarfs, giants, players, learned pig,
With other creatures odd;
The Dee brought cargoes rich with cakes.
And with them Mary Dod.

When Mary first approach'd the place.
To get on shore was trying;'
That she was there, on every voice.
Through all the Wake was flying.

A crowd collected — bought her cakes
They gaz'd till they were weary,
And they who'd of the Mammoth read;
Concluded it was Mary.

Her waist, what Muse can measure that;

Her arms were those of Chudleigh;
Her face — the moon when at the full,
Yet sweet as that of Sedley.

Had MARY been a Prussian born,
An equal mountain lov'd,
The human breed, like modern beef,
Had been in size improv'd.

A Brother MARY has, and he
Has wit and fat a quantum;
He lives, and is even now the pride
Of Britain's Troynobantum.

She also shows a Sister's claim,
To one that honours Leicester,
And folk will fully grant a right
Of which they can't divest her-

A Sister too and Mary boasts,
A race beyond reproach,
Since London laugh'd from end to end
When she o'erturn'd a coach.

With this huge tale, from Lombard-street,
The various mails went loaden,
And Fletcher told it in a trice,
To all the West, and Snowdon.

An Essex Cousin once was her's,
But Death, that chief of gaolers,
In mercy to the trade, entombed
This terror of the tailors,

The Sands of Dee

From Hoylake hall to Gayton come
Fine ladies — gentlemen;
They come my friends, to look at you
And you may look at them

And he that sightless leads the band,
When youth and mirth advance;
While Charity and Health draw near.
To bless—enjoy the dance.

Nor you degrade your country's name.
With base unsocial blow;
But save them — save the sinewy arm
For Britain's faithless foes.

On frumenty that day devoured;
The Muse is not enlarging.
But places that, with other freaks,
A rustic row, per margin.

And Mersey's waves brought him that bear
On every page the palm;
Uniting Wisdom's other name
With Gilead's healing balm.

And TRUMAN always joins the host
Where Fun's bright cup o'erflows;
For Cheshire, when she cheers her sons.
To him resigns their woes.

De Linden also crossed the Dee,
And brought his magic rods;
A foreign figure—thoughtful—thin,
No kin of Mary Dod's.

He likewise came, whose monstrous maw,
All Wales with terror fills;
They dread his drawing near the coast,
Lest he should eat their hills.

A Graham too, that favoured wight.
So oft consign'd to earth;
For what to other men is- deaths
To him is still a birth.

No Bishop, Judge, or sullen Saint,
Retains his serious powers.
O'er such a crop of living lumps.
Or talking cauliflowers.

'Tis true no Katterfelto comes,
With jetty puss arid passes;
This German only shew his grubs
To scientific classes.

Ne'er envy these my humble friends;
Nor thus disperse your groats,
Or else you'll think, in every drop,
A Wake gone down your throats.

Never for disgusting things,
With prying eyes explore,
But rummage Comfort's, every hoard,
And magnify her store.

And thank your stars that Mersey's stream,
For once denied assistance;
That friendly walls confined a fiend.

The Vulture at a distance.

From such a craw all Gayton's crowd
Would scamper off in haste;
To him, even Mary's solid self\
Would hardly be a taste.

Yet he drew nigh that travels — holds
At every wake his station,
As other Bears, set out from hence,
To close their education.

He goes with tardy minuet step,
At eve to meet the morrow;
The days that you devote to joy.
To him are days of sorrow.

From Torture's tricks disgusted turn,
My rural friends refrain;
shun the laugh, however loud.
That owes its birth to pain.

Humanity — dear harmless Dame,
ne'er her precepts break;
Still he her voice, and Heaven is your's,
A BLEST ETERNAL WAKE.

So shall the Muse, that means you well;
Has all your hopes at heart.
For you to Day's illustrious source,
An ardent prayer impart.

Phoebus, may I ask a boon,
For those that till the soil;

The worthiest part of human kind,
The humble sons of toil.

It is, that when through Night's dark shades,
Thy opening splendours break;
Thy brightest warmest beams may shine,
Wherever there's a Wake.

These days but seldom come to bring
To them, their annual glee;
bless them, and the eve shall close.
With songs of praise to thee.

And Lore, who likes to see old Night
Her ebon curtain spread,
Intreats, that on the coming mom.
Thy steeds lie long abed.

All Britain's every patron saint.
Shall join his wish to mine,
That endless youth— a glorious course,
A Giant's joy be thine.

Now wearied Health sat down to rest,
Even Mirth reclined her limbs,
And Gayton's festival day
Is closed — with all its whims.

Thus passes Life — a lengthened Day,
No power can time retard;
Where busy Tyre was life and glee,
Now — not a voice is heard…

The day wax'd short — the Wake grew thin,

Some sail'd adown the Dee,
While others tugg'd against the tide,
And row'd to Hilburee...

Appendix 5: William and Mary

As William and Mary walk'd by the sea side,
Their last farewell to take,
'Should you never return, young William' she said,
My poor heart will surely break'

'Be not thus dismay'd,' young William he said,
As he press'd the dear maid to his side,
'Nor my absence don't mourn, for when I return
I will make little Mary my bride.'

Three years pass'd by without any news,
When at last, as she sat at her door,
An old beggar came by, with a patch on his eye,
Quite lame, and did pity implore.

Mary started and trembled, 'Oh tell me' she cried,
'All the money I've got I will give.
Oh this I do ask you, if you will tell me true,
Only say, does my dear William live?

'Oh, I love him so dear, so true and sincere,
That no other I swear beside,
If in riches he rolled, and was he cloth'd in gold,
Should make little Mary his bride,'

'Forgive me, dear maid,' then William he said,
'Your love it was only I tried,
To church let's away, for e'er the sun sets,
I'll make little Mary my bride.'

ABOUT THE AUTHOR

Gavin Chappell was born in northern England and lives near Liverpool. After studying English at the University of Wales, he has since worked variously as a business analyst and a college lecturer. He is the author of numerous short stories, articles, poems and several books including *Wirral Smugglers, Wreckers and Pirates.*

Printed in Great Britain
by Amazon